THE ILLUSTRATED ENCYCLOPAEDIA OF COSTUME AND FASHION

THE ILLUSTRATED ENCYCLOPAEDIA OF COSTUME AND FASHION

FROM 1066 TO THE PRESENT

JACK CASSIN-SCOTT

First Published in Great Britain in 1994 by Studio Vista
This edition first published in 2006 by Cassell Illustrated
a division of Octopus Publishing Group Ltd.
2-4 Heron Quays, London E14 4JP

British Library Cataloguing-in-Publication Data
A catalogue entry for this title is available
from the British Library

Distributed in the United States
by Sterling Publishing Co., Inc
387 Park Avenue South, New York, NY 10016-8810

ISBN-13: 978-1-844034-83-3
ISBN-10: 1-84403-4-83-6
10 9 8 7 6 5 4 3 2 1

Printed in China

Contents

Sources of Illustrations in the Plates

1 Almark Publishing. **2** Strutt. **3** *Zur Geschichte der Köstume*. **4** Westminster Abbey. **5** After MS. British Museum. **6** After MS. British Museum. **7** Academy of Fine Arts Venice and British Museum. **8** *Zur Geschichte der Kostüme* and A. Dürer. **9** *Zur Geschichte der Kostüme* and Osprey. **10** After Holbein. Vienna and National Gallery, London. **11** Bronzine and Hans Eworth. **12** Titian and George Gower. **13** Barthol Bruyn and Hans Eworth. **14** Cornelis Ketel and Pantoja de la Cruz. **15** Antonio Moro and an Unknown Flemish Artist. **16** Francois Clouet and National Trust, Shrewsbury. **17** Alonzo Sanchez Coello. **18** Contemporary Continental Sources. **19** Contemporary Continental Sources. **20** Pantoja de la Cruz. **21** Pourbus and an Unknown Artist. **22** Isaac Oliver and The Costume Museum, London. **23** Daniel Mytens and *Zur Geschichte der Kostüme*. **24** Reubens and Contemporary Continental Sources. **25** Van Dyck and Gerard Honthorst. **26** Contemporary Continental Sources. **27** Diego de Silva Velázquez. **28** Contemporary Continental Sources. **29** Abraham Bosse and Gerard Honthorst. **30** Van Dyck and Daniel Mytens. **31** Meissonier and an Unknown Artist. **32** Wenceslaus Hollar and Engraving of the 17th century. **33** Diego de Silva Velázquez. **34** Van Dyck. **35** Van Dyck. **36** Wenceslaus Hollar. **37** Wenceslaus Hollar and Daniel Mytens. **38** Wenceslaus Hollar and Contemporary Continental Sources. **39** Van Dyck. **40** Wenceslaus Hollar. **41** Gerard ter Borch and Wenceslaus Hollar. **42** J.C. Meyern and Wenceslaus Hollar. **43** Diego de Silva Velázquez. **44** A. Van Tempel. **45** Gerard ter Borch. **46** Netscher. **47** I.D. Saint-Jean and Gerard ter Borch. **48** Bonnart and I.D. de Saint-Jean. **49** I.D. de Saint-Jean. **50** I.D. de Saint-Jean and Contemporary Continental Sources. **51** Hyacinthe Rigaud and I.D. de Saint-Jean. **52** I.D. de Saint-Jean and Contemporary Continental Sources. **53** Trouvain and I.D. de Saint-Jean. **54** Largillière and an Unknown Artist. **55** Bonnard and Contemporary Continental Sources. **56** *Zur Geschichte der Kostüme* and an Unknown Artist. **57** Jodokus Verbeek. **58** Contemporary Continental Sources and Temple Newsom House, Leeds. **59** Godfrey Kneller. **60** Richard Waitt and Contemporary Continental Sources. **61** William Hogarth and Contemporary Continental Sources. **62** Hèrriset.**63** Alan Ramsay. **64** An original specimen at The Gallery of the English Costume, Manchester. **65** William Hogarth. **66** François Boucher. **67** Arthur Devis and Adolphe Menzel. **68** Adolph Menzel and Henry Pickering. **69** *Taylors Complete Guide*, 1796. **70** Continental lithograph, c. 1765. **71** Victoria and Albert Museum, 1760–70. **72** After Calet, 1775. **73** *Journal des Luxus und der Moden*, 1786. **74** After Lister, 1789. **75** *Mode in Costume*, Wilcox, 1789. **76/77** *Journal des Luxus und der Moden*, 1790–91. **78** *Costume Cavalcade* and *Journal des Luxus und der Moden*, 1792. **79** *Journal des Luxus und der Moden*, 1792. **80** After N. Heideloff, 1794. **81** *Journal der Luxus und der Moden*, 1793. **82** After Vernet, 1793. **83** After Vernet and Tresca, 1795. **84** *Journal der Luxus und der Moden*, 1800. **85** *La Mesangère*, 1800. **86** *Journal des Modes*, 1801. **87** *Journal des Dames*, 1805. **88** *Journal des Dames*, 1809. **89** *Mode in Costume*, Wilcox. **90/91** *Journal des Dames and allgemeine Mode*, 1810/11/12/13. **92** *La Mesangère*. 1814. **93** *Journal des Dames*, 1815. **94** *Journal des Dames* and *Lady's Magazine*, 1818. **95** *Lady's Magazine*, 1820. **96** *Allgemeine Modezeitung*, 1822. **97** *Concise History of Costume*, Laver, 1826. **98** *Journal des Dames*, 1826. **99** *Journal des Dames et des Modes*, 1829. **100** *Journal des Dames et des Modes*, 1831. **101** *Concise History of Costume*, Laver, 1831. **102** *Allgemeine Modezeitung, 1833*. **103** *Allgemeine Modezeitung*, 1834. **104** *Monthly Belle Assemble*, 1836/1837. **105** *La Mode*, 1836 and *Monthly Belle Assemble*, 1836. **106/107** *Mode de Paris*, 1838. **108** *Journal des Dames et des Modes*, 1840/41. **109** *Allgemeine Modezeitung*, 1840. **110** *Le Bon Ton*, 1839. **111** *Journal des Dames*, 1842. **112** *Allgemeine Modezeitung*, 1844. **113** *Le Folet*, c. 1846. **114** *Cut of Men's Clothes*, 1846. **115** *Allgemeine Modezeitung*, 1848. **116** *Le Moniteur de le Mode*, 1849. **117** *Allgemeine Modezeitung*, 1850. **118** *Allgemeine Modezeitung*, 1851. **119** *Weiner Elegante*, 1852. **120** *Cut of Women's Clothes*, 1855, child's fashion, 1852. **121** Continental lithograph, c. 1860. **122/123** *Penelope, der Bazar* and continental lithograph, 1855/57. **124** *Costume Cavalcade*, 1857. **125** Continental lithograph, c. 1860. **126** *Magazine de Demoiselles*, 1860. **127** *Magazine de Demoiselles*, 1862. **128** *Magazine des Demoiselles*, 1862. **129** Continental lithograph, c. 1863. **130** *Allgemeine Modezeitung, 1865*. **131** After Tissot, 1873. **132** Continental lithograph, c. 1876. **133** Continental lithograph, c. 1876. **134** Continental lithograph, c. 1879. **135** Continental lithograph, c. 1880. **136** Continental lithograph, c. 1881. **137** Continental lithograph, c. 1884. **138/139** American and continental lithographs, 1885/87. **140** Continental lithograph, c. 1887. **141** *Costume Cavalcade*, 1888. **142** *Der Bazar*, 1893. **143** *Cut of Women's Clothes*, 1894. **144** *Cassels Magazine*, 1895. **145** *Cassels Magazine*, 1895. **146** *Cassels Magazine*, 1895. **147** *Cassels Magazine*, 1896. **148** *Cassels Magazine*, 1896. **149** *Cassels Magazine*, 1897. **150** After Reznicek, 1899. **151** *Cut of Women's Clothes*, 1903. **152/153** *Illustrierte Frauenzeitung* and *Journal des Dames*, 1908/9. **154** *Die Dame*, 1912. **155** *Journal des Demoiselles*, 1912. **156** *Les Modes and die Dame*, 1913. **157** *Die Dame*, 1915. **158** *Die Dame*, 1917. **159** *Vogue*, 1918 and *Wiener Modezeitung*, 1918. **160** *Cut of Women's Clothes* and the *Tailor and Cutter*, 1920s. **161** After Erté. **162** After Erté. **163** Princes Street Parade and Krize 1928. **164** George Newnes Ltd. **165** Princes Street Parade and Tailor and Cutter. **166** Mainbocher. **167** Magnone and Armed Forces of Second World War. **168** *Vogue* and Victoria & Albert Museum. **169** Dior and Fath. **170** Fenez. **171** Givenchy and Dior. **172** Yves St Laurent and Pucci. **173** Yves St Laurent. **174** Yves St Laurent and Cardin. **175** Peter Max. **176** Féraud, Givenchy and Aquascutum. **177** Mary Quant. **178** Valentino and Yves St Laurent. **179** Mary Quant, Giorgio Armani and Torrente. **180** Chanel and Yves St Laurent.

Glossary

Aiglets Metal tags used to join sleeves and hose to doublet

Aigrettes Standing plume of feathers worn on the head

A la chinoise Hair pulled tightly back at sides of head into knot held with an ornamental pin or bow at back

A la titus Cropped hairstyle supposed to resemble locks of condemned victims awaiting execution by guillotine

A la madonna Hair parted in middle with ringlets or curls at either side

A sous pieds Trousers or pantaloons fastening under the foot

Bagwig Queue of wig placed in black silk bag at nape of neck

Baldrick Wide sash of silk or leather, worn over right shoulder, supporting a sword

Band strings Usually tasselled ties for fastening ruffs in front

Banyan Loose coat worn indoors, usually of washable material

Barbette Piece of white linen worn over the head and under the chin

Basque Very short overskirt sewn on to bodice

Bavolet Short veil attached to back of bonnet, shading neck

Bents Strips of bone or wood to distend farthingales

Bertha Deep collar of lace or silk worn around neck and shoulders

Betsie Small neck ruff of fine lawn or lace

Bicorne Man's hat turned up at front and back forming points either side

Bishop sleeve Lady's day sleeve with full shoulder, gathered in to wrist cuff

Bombast Padding and stuffing to distend garments

Bongrace Oblong stiffened head piece projecting over forehead

Brandenburgs Ornamental fastenings or braided loops and buttons

Brutus Roman-style, untidy haircut

Buff coat Sleeveless military coat of ox hide

Buffon Gauze, linen or lace neckerchief

Bum roll Padded roll for distending hips

Burnous Mantle with hood influenced by Arabian garment of same name

Buskin Close-fitting, calf-length boot, usually of leather

Bustle Pad worn underneath skirt to extend contour of hips at back

Cadogan Male: hairstyle with two horizontal curled rolls above ears and queue the back. Female: large bun the back of neck held in place by net or ribbon

Calash Large folding hood of whalebone or cane hoops, covered in silk

Calotte Close-fitting man's cap with chin ties.

Campaign wigs Military type wigs with short side locks and short queue behind

Canezou Bodice with high neckline and long sleeves

Canions Extensions from trunk hose to knees

Capote Ornate bonnet with ribbon bows tying at sides or front

Capuchin collar Continuous rolled collar

Caraco Woman's thigh-length jacket worn with long petticoat

Carmagnole Peasant jacket

Cartwheel ruff Large stiffly starched collar

Castellated Decorative slashings of edges of garments, into square cut edges

Caul Cap of silk or gold thread network, often silk lined

Cavalier hat Type of hat worn by English Royalists

Caxon wig (or tie wig) Worn for undress and usually white

Chapeau bras Tiny tricorn hat carried under arm when wigs and headdresses were very large

Chaperone Headdress combining hood and small shoulder cape

Chemise Undergarment of linen worn by male and female

Chemisette Tulle, cambric or muslin covering to decolletage

Cherusque Standing ruff collar made of lace

Chevrons V-shaped motif made of woven cloth, denoting rank of an NCO (non-commissioned officer).

Cloak bag breeches Baggy, oval shaped breeches fitted just above knee

Cod-piece Small bag formed at the fork of men's hose; Spanish origin

Coif Bonnet type close fitting cap

Copotain hat Hat with a high conical crown with a narrow brim

Cornet hat Made of lace, and worn in various styles as a day cap

Cotehardie Outer garment

D.A. Haircut in the shape of a duck's rear worn by Teddy Boys

Décolletage Low neckline of a lady's dress

Demi-gigot Sleeve full from shoulder to elbow, then tight to the wrist

Doublet Bombast jacket usually close fitting and waisted

Dundreary Hairstyle with wide whiskers

Echelles Stomacher trimmed down front with ribbon bows

Engageantes Ruffles of lace showing at cuff of dress

Epaulette Collar, often of lace, frequently covering shoulders

Escarpins Low-cut flat slippers

Falling band collar Collar which lay on shoulders without support

***Fanchon* bonnet** Small day-time cap

Farthingale or verdingale Structure expanding skirt by hoops of bone, wood, etc.

Fedora Velour hat with fairly high tapering crown

Fichu Triangular piece of material draped over low neckline

Finestrella Slashed sleeves

Fontange Linen cap with tall erections of lace or linen frills supported by wire frame

Forage cap Side hat worn by the military

French hood Small bonnet worn at back of head with front border curving round the ears

Frogging Decorative loop fastenings for coat

Full-bottomed wig Shoulder length large wig with centre parting and curls framing face

Furbelow Deep, puckered flounce

Gaiter Covering for instep or ankle, sometimes extending to knees

Gallouses Braces (suspenders USA)

Gigot **(leg-o'-mutton)** Sleeves, very wide at shoulder, tapering gradually to wrist

Glen Urquhart Scottish tartan of dark blue, dark green and black overlaid with a fine red line crossing at right angles in a box formation

Godet Tapering pleat expanding downwards to give a flared effect

Goffered Describes pleated muslin for the neck or sleeve

Golillia Spanish for standing collar round back of head

Greaves Leggings of metal or leather

Guards Borders either plain or decorated to conceal seams

Gun club Pattern produced in worsted, flannel and tweed in checks of different colours and alternating rows

Hanger type sword Worn from waist belt and frog, usually worn under coat

Headrail Headdress of linen or cotton worn by Anglo-Saxon women

Hot pants Brief version of shorts

Houppelande Style of dress for both sexes, worn both long and short

Jabot Full frill at neck, knotted at back, sometimes worn with ornamental pin at throat

Jacquard Knitting stitch with a raised motif

Jockei Short oversleeve

Justaucorps French name for man's close-fitting coat worn over waistcoat

Kimono sleeve Wide hanging sleeves, sometimes hanging longer at back

Kirtle Underskirt

Knickerbockers Full, knee-length breeches

Landknect Swiss and German mercenary soldiers

Lappet Lace or linen pieces attached to cap, usually hanging down on either side of face

Macaroni Young man dressed in extreme of fashion 1770-80

Mameluke Full sleeve tied in puffs at intervals from shoulder to wrist

Mantelet Shawl worn around shoulders

Mantilla Veil taped over head or shoulder; Spanish origin

Mantua gown Loose unboned bodice gown worn with open front revealing petticoat and fitted with long train

Medici collar Standing collar round back of neck and made from net or lace

Mentonnières Frills round inside of bonnet, framing face

Muscadin Dandy of 1790s, named after scented pastille of musk which he carried

Négligée Term used by male and female for informal dress

Nether stocks Lower stocking portion of hose

Pagoda sleeve Funnel-shaped sleeve, tight from shoulder to elbow, then widening to wrist with ruffles

Pallatine Shoulder wrap for ladies

Panes Produced either by slashing or strips of ribbon set close together

Pannier French for the side hoops

Pantaloons Long, tight trousers

Pantalettes Separate leg coverings with ruffles that extend below hem of dress

Parti-coloured tights Close fitting tights of silk or cloth, with legs of different colours

Partlet Type of chemisette or 'fill in' for low decolletage

Pattens Overshoe footwear made of wood and raised by iron stand

Peascod belly Formed by padding front of doublet and overhanging girdle

Pelerine Shoulder cape, often with long ends hanging down front

Pelisse Cape, often fur-trimmed

Phrygian cap Tall hat worn by Anglo-Saxons, then by French Revolutionaries.

Pickadils Tabbed or scalloped order on doublet skirts and as supports for ruff

Pinner Lappets of cap being pinned up; later plain cap with frill

Plastron False front, simulating blouse or waistcoat

Pluderhose German for wide baggy trunk-hose

Points Ties used to attach male trunk-hose to doublet and female sleeves and gowns

Polonaise Woman's gown with close-fitting bodice and full skirt, looped up to form three drapes, worn over separate skirt

Pommander Suspended receptacle for perfume

Poulaine/Cracowe Long-pointed shoes worn by dandies of the 14th century

Princess line Dress without seam at back

Punk Cult of bizarre, aggressively dressed young people

Queue Hanging tail of wig

Redingote Waisted coat with large collar and revers, single or double breasted with cut-away tails

Redingote dress Dress with lapels and front opening on skirt

Rhinegrave ('Petticoat breeches') In style of divided skirt decorated with ribbon bows

Ribbon knots Clusters of various coloured ribbon loops, worn by both sexes

Ribbon loops Usually in clusters and on both male and female costumes

Robings Flat trimmings decorating gown round neck and front of bodice

Sabretache Small, embroidered handbag of military origin

Sack gown Loose gown of box pleats sewn into back, from neck line to shoulder

Slashings Symmetrical arrangement of slits in various lengths, with pulled through lining as decoration

Slop hose Wide breeches effected by sailors but civilian fashion in 16th and 17th centuries

Solitaire Wide, black ribbon worn around the neck, tying on to the wig

Soutache Flat narrow cord used for decorative motifs

Spencer Short, tight jacket

Steinkirk Long cravat, loosely knotted, ends threaded through buttonhole or pinned to one side; Worn by both sexes

Stock Close-fitting wide neckcloth

Stuart cap Cap which formed a widow's peak in front and slightly curved at sides

Surcoat First worn over armour, then used for fashion for both sexes

Sweet gloves Scented Spanish leather gloves

Tablier Descending trimmings on gown, suggesting decorative apron

Taffeta pipkin Small hat with flat crown drawn into narrow brim

Tippet Short shoulder cape, originally a mediaeval liripipium

Toque Brimless cap

Tricorne A three-cornered hat

Trunk hose Extended portion of male leg-wear from waist, joining stockings at fork

Trunk sleeves ('Cannon sleeves') Wide at top becoming close-fitting to waist

Ulster coat Double-breasted coat, fitted with several capes

Underpropper Wire structure fixed at back of neck to support large ruff

Vandyke beard Fashion worn at the time as painted by the artist Van Dyck

Venetian breeches Wide pear-shaped padded hose which reached and fastened just below knee

Void shoes Broad, open-slashed flat shoes

Wings Projections over shoulder seams of doublets or bodices

Introduction

In the study and appreciation of costume, it is a general impression of fashion which reveals the true sense of the period. Each country adopted the technical 'know how' of others to express an improvement of their own costume.

The aim of this book is to highlight those points of fashion which express change in style over a period of nearly a thousand years. The illustrations, based on contemporary sources, provide a fascinating and intriguing visual insight into the social and psychological reasons for fashion.

During the eleventh century, clothes did not vary to any great extent in shape or style, merely being worn in various ways. Tunics were common and were worn by most people, but the fabric and length depended on the social standing of the wearer – from long, silken tunics from the East for the wealthy to short, home-spun coarse-cloth tunics for the poor.

Throughout the Middle Ages costume for ladies of the court became more ornate, due to the influences of the Eastern materials brought back by the Crusaders. Male costume changed radically at this period, the result of Italian influences whose styles gained great popularity. But as with all fashion, this was short-lived. In due course a fashion for women emerged that aimed to cover the body completely.

In the sixteenth century, the influence of the Spanish court fashion was more then merely that of fashionable trends, it also had great political basis. The powerful Spanish Empire, which embraced much of Europe, the New Americas and Africa, made the Spanish presence felt. The stiff silhouette of this fashion caused the functional purpose of the costume to be of little importance, it was the decorative effect, with the costume merely the background for the encrusted jewel design of wealth.

France inaugurated the greatest changes against the artificiality of Spanish fashion and by 1625 had completely changed the silhouette of both male and female. Out went the bombast and stiffness of the Spanish style and into fashion came soft folds and draperies, with a greater accent on mobility by casting aside the farthingale and stomacher. These were replaced with a higher waistline, and loose falling skirts with lace or ribbon instead of precious stones and whalebone.

The development of men's fashion was more intriguing, the masculine costumes being generally replaced by more effeminate clothing. The excessive trimmings of ribbon loops on the wide Rhinegraves breeches, gave the ludicrous effect of petticoats.

Another French influence of this period was the introduction of the wig, which became the symbol of the aristocracy; it typified the ruling classes. At this time women wore long wig curls, but never reached the splendour of the male wig. The female answer was the high *Fontange* of wired upstanding lace or ribbon.

The extravagant styles of this Baroque era were gradually replaced by a more elegant dignity. Making its appearance in male fashion was the *Justaucorps* the waistcoat and breeches being the forerunner of the male suit. In women's fashion the skirt lengthened into a train at the back revealing the underskirt, the drapery being gathered behind on a supporting frame giving the first 'bustle' effect. The first Rococo era (1760 to 1789) was based upon a style of European art originating in France and combined irregularity of form with a lavish freedom of elegant design. Women's wigs reached fantastic heights.

With the passing of the Revolution (1789 to 1794) and the beginning of the Directoire (1795), a more fascinating period of French fashion began. Characteristic of this era was the high waistline of women's clothing which remained throughout the Empire period. A new simplicity of fashion was reflected in the long white gowns which became very fashionable and the flimsy transparent ones which became universal.

In the Napoleonic era, Empress Josephine led the court in the splendour of her fashion. Although having an effect on French fashion prior to the Revolution, English tailoring continued to influence the development of men's clothing. The English dandy George 'Beau' Brummell (1778 to 1840) brought the English cut to perfection.

The age of the Romantics was an era of novelists and poets, and the return of the noble *émigré* and the Royal Family to Paris. The long sheath and high waist disappeared from women's fashion; lightly corseted waists re-emerged. Male fashion sported a wide range of coats and informally appeared in bright, striped trousers.

From about 1840 to 1870, Rococo underwent a revival with the rebirth of the crinoline. Also the introduction of the sewing machine began to make clothes more widely available.

The Victorian age saw the first move towards the emancipation of women, but the emphasis was still on ornamentation and accessories. In men's clothes there was a trend for more sombreness in style and new manufacturing methods rapidly gaining ground. The twentieth century brought the *belle époque* and the Edwardian era, the age of the 'Gibson Girl' then evolving into more sweeping changes initiated around 1910 by Paul Poiret and other designers.

Following the international upheavals and repercussions of the First World War, fashions changed drastically. Men's clothes became more standard in appearance, with sports and the new activity of motoring dictating fashion. In women's clothes came the greatest change; the 1920's saw the tubular silhouette and a more masculine approach to fashion. The slender silhouette became popular, with waistlines falling to the hips and hemlines rising to the knees. With the 'Roaring Twenties' came the flattened bust line, giving a boyish look. The fashionable cloche hat fitted perfectly the bobbed or shingled hairstyles.

The decade of the thirties swept aside the slender masculine styles and brought back the bustline and longer skirts, from knee to mid-calf. The Hollywood film world dominated the high fashion of the thirties. The 'Stars of the Silver Screen' replaced the society ladies who had previously inspired fashionable trends.

The forties and the Second World War had a drastic effect on fashion. Designs became slimmer in silhouette, with much less material being used due to shortages. Millions of women wore uniforms in the service of their country. At the end of the war a reaction in fashion, the 'New Look', an ultra-feminine style with full, long skirts, arrived.

Clothes in the early fifties were less formal than they had been before 1939, but women began to move back to more elegant styles. Many pre-war trends were revived and modified. Men followed with the Edwardian look. The 'Teddy Boy' suit remained, however, a fashion seen lower down the social scale.

The Swinging Sixties made their mark on the lighter side of fashion with the 'Dolly Girl' and her mini-dresses. Ethnic and see-through styles also made their appearance. Gradually the designers brought in more formal designs with frilly feminine styles and trouser suits. Jeans also became more acceptable and popular.

The early seventies brought no dramatic changes; the basic silhouette of the calf-length midi remained in fashion, with variations. The 'maxi' length became popular, and denim jeans influenced fashion. During this decade the 'country look' in casual clothes became a trend which continued through the next decade.

The eighties saw a continuation of styles from previous years. 'Punk' remained a strong influence, but this aggressive fashion lost much of its impact once it became more generally accepted (in modern fashion, high street styles are usually about a year to eighteen months behind designer outfits). The use in designs of 'Pop Art' and Picasso-style art became a fashion trend at the end of the decade and the start of the nineties.

This is the cavalcade of changing fashion, limited inevitably by the confines of a book, yet nonetheless fascinating in its visual impact.

1066-1550

1 Anglo Saxon 'thegn' and Norman soldier, c. 1066

The fashions of the Anglo-Saxons followed a similar pattern to those of the earlier Roman civilization in Britain. The upper-class Anglo-Saxon 'thegn' (left) wore linen shirts and loose, long, leather-belted trousers, either cross-gartered or stuffed into soft leather high boots. Over these was a tunic, generally knee-length and long-sleeved with a round neck. A super-tunic on top reached just above the knees; this was encircled with a stout leather belt. The rectangular or semi-circular cloak was fastened on the right shoulder by a brooch. The tallish hat known as a phrygian cap was made from wool or leather, and in wartime was reinforced with iron.

Anglo-Saxons and Normans, close neighbours, adopted many elements of each other's dress, varying only in minor details and hairstyles. The loose-fitting shirt of the Norman Soldier (right) had long, close, tight sleeves which wrinkled to the wrist, and the rounded neckline was drawn in. On top was a knee-length short-sleeved tunic. Both neckline and sleeve edges bore coloured embroidery. The legs were covered by long breeches or braies of wool or cloth, sometimes worn loose. Here they are bound with leather thonging or cloth strips. Over these garments were wide, short breeches which reached the knees like a divided skirt. On the feet were simple, low-cut shoes in leather, canvas or felt. The typical Norman hairstyle is cropped short, especially at the back – useful under an iron war helmet.

2 Upper-class man and woman, c. 1075

The women of this period dressed simply. They wore a long under-tunic with floor-length skirts; the sleeves were long and close-fitting to the wrist. Over this under-tunic or gown was worn an over-tunic, which fell to just below knee length; it had wide, elbow-length sleeves and was drawn in at the natural waist by a girdle. This over-tunic was embroidered down the centre front from the neckline to the hem, and round the hem. The cuff of the three-quarter sleeve was likewise embroidered. The hair was always covered: this lady is wearing a veil or headrail which entirely conceals her hair. The short white veil was put over the head and crossed over on the left shoulder; the front edge of the veil hung over the forehead in small pleats. The feet were covered by soft leather low-heeled shoes.

Upper-class men adopted a long full white tunic which fell to the ground in heavy folds. A stiff, embroidered collar covers the rounded neckline of the tunic. The sleeves were long to the wrist and close-fitting, and cut in one with the tunic. The voluminous rectangular or semi-circular cloak, not unlike a Roman toga, was wrapped around the body and cast over the left shoulder. It too was edged with embroidery. On the feet were worn similar shoes to those of the women, low-cut in soft leather.

3 Knight and lady, c. 1195

The knights of this period wore an all-enveloping chain mail coat and leg covering with armoured leg greaves. A helmet similar to the Greek/Roman style was often worn, although this was often a personal choice of the wearer. At this time they were frequently made from leather, but later from iron. These helmets were worn over a hood of chain mail which can be seen swathed around the neck of the knight. On the surcoat or cyclas is emblazoned the knight's insignia – in this case lions. The surcoat came to just below knee length and was slit at the sides. Attached at either shoulder was a large, all-covering cloak. Around the waist of the surcoat was a leather belt, from which hung attached the heavy sword. Long hair, beards and moustaches were a very popular fashion at this period.

Here is a fashionable young lady of the twelfth century, wearing an undergarment consisting of a long, loose gown falling in folds to the ground, with long, close-fitting sleeves. From rounded neckline to hem it was covered in a simple coloured design. The sleeveless, open-sided overgarment reached well below knee level, remaining loose and flowing; this too was covered in a simple design such as the diaper pattern shown here. Shoes were of soft leather and embroidered. This young woman's unbound hair was allowed to hang flowing down at the back; alternatively it could be worn in two long plaits, sometimes covered in long silk casings. A simple jewelled headband adorned the hairline.

4 Man and woman, c. 1269

A simple fashionable costume for men at this time was the loose, open-at-the-neck tunic. The tunic itself was cut wide, with close-fitting sleeves to the wrist. This wide-in-the-body tunic could be long or short; shown here is the calf-length style, with a narrow leather belt at the waist. Tight hose of cloth or silk were worn, sewn to the shape of the leg. The shoes were of soft leather, with peaked fronts sometimes two inches beyond the toe. The long hair and beard were popular styles.

Women wore a loose, full-length undergarment with long, tight sleeves, usually made in a rich material; over this was worn another gown with a round neckline. This gown was still loose, flowing and floor-length, but was now beginning to be more fitted to the figure; it had close-fitting, three-quarter length sleeves which revealed the undergarment sleeve. This overgarment formed a short train at the back and was sometimes held up in front, both to aid walking and to reveal the rich material of the undergarment. Headgear consisted of the barbette, a band of linen, worn with a goffered fillet – a development of the previously plain linen headband. The barbette was placed under the chin with the ends resting on top of the head. The head was then encased with a goffered fillet, the female version of the coif. An amply cut, rich, full, loose cloak, with ribbon tiers to hold it together over the shoulders, was draped over the gown. Shoes were in soft leather.

5 Man and woman, c. 1377

The eccentricities of fashion are depicted here with the man's houppelande or pelican. This was a loose, baggy garment in either a long or short fashion. Illustrated is the extremely short version. Sleeves were long, opening to a wide cuff at the wrist. The high collar, coming up to the back of the head, was fastened to the chin in front, although the collar was often turned down. The tunic was fastened about the waist with an ornamental leather belt. This was the period of the absurd fashion of wearing long peaked-toe shoes called Poulaine or Cracowe. For walking they had to be tied just below the knees with gold chains. They were made in various materials; the toes were sometimes stuffed hard with hair, wool or even moss, and sometimes left to hang limp.

Hairstyles for men were flowing and collar-length, curling at the ears and forehead. Fashionable men went clean-shaven.

Women followed the simple fashion of the close-fitting cotehardie or underdress, consisting of an all-in-one skirt and bodice buttoned in front and with an open, round neckline. The skirt was full and long to the ground. Sleeves were close-fitting to the wrist, ornamented with buttons from elbow to hand. A girdle, similar to the man's belt, was worn at hip height. The surcoat was a long, sleeveless garment open from the shoulder to the top of the thigh. Through the opening was revealed the cotehardie and hip belt. The edges were often fur-trimmed. The hair was completely hidden by the pearl- and gold-embroidered caul, over which was attached an ornamental padded roll.

6 French or Flemish man and woman, c. 1480

In French/Flemish high fashion of this period the women wore a black velvet hood with a head crown, the whole pinned with a large side brooch. The long, full gown had a convex neckline showing an edge of the white chemise beneath. The fitted waistline was encircled with a belt. The long skirts were lifted and fastened at the back, revealing a contrasting coloured kirtle. The sleeves were long, projecting over the hands, with puffs of chemise showing through the slashings from the elbow down the forearm, and widening at the cuffs.

Women's fashions changed in style much more quickly than men's, which were now much plainer and cut higher at the neckline. The greatest change was the headdress: the head was now enveloped in concealing bonnets and hoods. Fashionable men wore big beaver hats adorned with very large feathers, tied on with a coloured scarf over a close-fitting cap. The knee-length jacket had a wide, flat collar with revers of fur. The hanging sleeves were slit up the seam to allow the arm to come through. Encircling the waist was a fine belt which supported a fancy tasselled pouch. Dark grey hose were worn under shoes with thick, broad toes and a minimum of leather around the heels; the sole, too, narrowed at the heels.

7 Young Italian dandies, c. 1490

Towards the end of the fifteenth century young Italian dandies were wearing clothes so extravagant that they were close to fancy dress. Their short, open-type doublets (left), wide-cut, emphasised the chest, while a narrow waistline exposed the chemise front with its high neckline. Sleeves had puffed tops and were close-fitting below the elbow. Tight-fitting hose, sometimes parti-coloured, were worn beneath short overpants. Three-quarter length stockings were also worn. Shoes were now blunt-toed and wide-fitting, with low backs and open side pieces. Fancy leather belts girded the waist, carrying tasselled pouches and a sword. Coloured beaver hats with large feathers continued to be a highlight of fashion.

The Italian Renaissance high fashion allowed for the warmer climate of southern Europe. The high doublet collars of the previous style were never very popular, so the tunic was thrown open and the collar turned down (right). The belt was discarded, allowing the tunic to hang loose in folds and creating a square silhouette. The collar was in a contrasting colour to the tunic, and its centre opening revealed the chemise beneath. The wide sleeves allowed the close-fitting sleeve of the undergarment to be glimpsed, with puffs of chemise protruding through the slashings. The well-fitting parti-coloured hose were attached to the waist by tapes. Shoes were blunt-toed and cut low at the heel. A pillbox-shaped hat was in fashion and worn by most classes. A warm cloak or cape was a necessary accessory.

8 Italian and German ladies, c. 1495

In the Italian Renaissance style (left), women wore their hair completely or partially displayed. Curled blonde hair decorated with jewelled and flowered headbands was fashionable. From the very low-cut *décolletage* of the bodice and high waistline the Venetian silk gown fell in heavy folds to the ground. Its open slit front revealed the richly embroidered underskirt. The dress was often lifted up, both to aid walking and to expose a side view of the brocaded underskirt. The close-fitting slashed finestrella sleeves revealed the chemise through the slashings.

The German fashion (right) at this time was highlighted by the bulbous or jellybag form of head attire. Made from linen stitched in multiple rows to stiffen the band, it was often filled with tow or horsehair. A gauze veil fell from the headband to cover the eyebrows. The neckline of the gown was rounded and cut fairly low. The high-waisted bodice was small and close-fitting, with the skirt hanging in heavy folds to the ground. The sleeves were long and close-fitting below the elbow, coming over the hand, while the upper wings of the sleeve were puffed and slashed. At the elbow the sleeve was slashed to reveal large puffs of the under chemise. The gown needed to be lifted to assist the wearer in walking.

9 German/Swiss soldier and lady, and a Yeoman of the Guard, c. 1500

The German/Swiss mercenary soldiers known as *Landknecht* created a mixture of fashions, the remnants of their plunder, which were copied by fashionable young men. Their large-brimmed leather or felt hats were slashed, curled back and profusely decorated with feathers. The parti-coloured hose worn with ribboned garters below each knee were often slashed to reveal bare flesh. The doublet, of various colours, had very wide slashed sleeves caught in at the wrist. Scanty slashed hose pants were worn with a small cod-piece. Armoured breast plates were attached over these soldiers' doublets. Heavy swords were carried as tools of their trade. Square-toed shoes called void shoes were slashed and had narrow strap fastenings.

The ladies' large felt hats followed the *Landknecht* fashion. The hair beneath was gathered into a jewelled caul. The chemise was ruched and gathered into the neckline to achieve a deeply textured look similar to the slashings. From the high waistline the gown fell to the ground. The rich, heavy folds were pulled up at the front to reveal the undergarment. The wide chemise sleeves were drawn in tightly at the wrist. The most fashionable materials for the nobility were silks, velvets, taffetas and brocades in subdued dark greens and blues.

The horseman is a Yeoman of the Guard, dressed in the livery of the Tudors. His undershirt was cut low at the neck and then drawn together, ruching the material into close gathers. The over-tunic was short to the knees and richly ornamented with a Tudor rose on the chest; the square neckline and hem were edged with embroidery. The upper part of the tunic was parti-coloured. The full-shouldered sleeves tapered down to fit closely at the wrist, whose cuffs were embroidered like the collar and hem. The close-fitting flat linen cap or calotte was slashed, with chin tie strings attached. Tight-fitting hose were worn.

10 Court dress for men and women (Henry VIII and Jane Seymour), c. 1535

The courtiers of Henry VIII's reign wore a high-collared doublet, stuffed, padded and slashed to reveal white puffs of chemise. The slashings were interspersed with jewels and heavy embroidery. The vest was cut wide and low, above matching, knee-length skirts. Two white sashes encircled the waist, one carrying a dagger with gold mounts. The centre opening of the skirt revealed an elaborate cod-piece. Close-fitting white hose, the left one encircled with the royal garter, covered the legs. On the King's feet are slashed, short, square, spread-toed shoes rising over the instep to cover the feet. The voluminous gown was of red velvet lined with sable and heavily embroidered with gold cord. The unusable lower hanging sleeve was tubular and set at the back. The large puffed upper sleeve was gored and decorated in gold embroidery. The bonnet was of black felt with white plumage, and the underside of the turn-up was decorated with jewels. Henry wore a jewelled gold pendant and carried leather gloves.

Queen Jane Seymour is seen wearing headgear of the gable/kennel type, typical of this period. Both lappets of the coif were pinned up. The coronet or back curtain was split into two pieces and the right section twisted up at the back and pinned into a 'whelk-shell' shape; the left side carried over to hang over the right shoulder. The low, square neckline of the red velvet gown was decorated with pearl and ruby bands. The inverted V-shape of the skirt from the natural waistline opened down the front, revealing the embroidered underskirt which matches the large slashed false sleeves. The broad cuff was pinned back to the elbow. The bell shape of the farthingale was sometimes effected by pleating the material of the petticoats. The accessories consisted of rings and a magnificent pendant.

1550-1620

11 Lady of quality and boy, c. 1550

The lady is dressed in the English style of the period. The bodice was tight-fitting with a square yoke of darker colour, and had a high neck with a Medici collar. The high collar was closed by a gold jewelled 'choker' with a pendant hanging to the yoke. The sleeves were funnel shaped, close-fitting at the top, then expanding to a wide opening from the elbow. The undersleeves were trimmed with embroidered edgings and aiglets which, when fastened, closed the undersleeves. The skirt, in the Spanish farthingale style, had the forepart matching the undersleeves. The headwear was the English version of the French hood, made on a stiff base and worn close fitting towards the back of the head. It was curved forward to end just over the ears on either side, and the back raised into a horseshoe shape.

The boy wears the padded doublet. Although longer than in the previous period, it still retained the bulky appearance; the waistline being just above the hips. The doublet, sleeves and trunk hose were slashed, revealing patches of the chemise worn underneath. The jacket followed the shape of the doublet. The collar was turned down flat on the shoulders. The small bonnet with a full pleated crown was worn with a bunch of feathers. The shoes, matching the rest of the outfit, were decorated with slashings.

12 English lady and Spanish nobleman, c. 1553

The lady is wearing a high-necked, close-fitting gown with a small but closed-all-round ruff. The bodice was close-fitting and fairly rigid, with the waistline sloping to a deep V-shape point in front. A gored skirt expanded in a funnel shape without folds from the small tight waist to the ground. The sleeves had a welt which surrounded the armhole and formed a small wing effect. These sleeves were full from the shoulder to the wrist, finishing in a tight cuff from which extended a small wrist ruff. The close-fitting coif covered the hair, it was made from linen or other suchlike material. Over this was worn the 'bongrace'. This was usually made from stiffened velvet, oblong in shape and worn flat on the head.

The man wears a Spanish style with the body of the doublet, slightly formed in the peascod belly style. A high-standing collar was edged with a turned down border fashioned in pickadils to support a ruff. The doublet sleeves were close-fitting to the wrist ending in short wrist ruffs. The trunk hose had long slashes and were also ornamented with the fashionable cod-piece. The length of the gown reached just above the knees, and was usually worn open. Slashed shoes of soft leather, silk or velvet were worn.

13 Dutch and English ladies, c. 1557

The lady on the right is wearing a gown. This overgarment was worn on formal occasions, over the bodice and skirt. The loose-bodied gown had a high neck which was surmounted by a small ruff. Short, puffed-out shoulder sleeves to elbow length revealed the straight sleeves of the bodice, which ended in wrist ruffs. Fitting close to the shoulders, the gown, when fastened from the neck to the waist, formed a conical shape to the ground, leaving an inverted V-shape opening from the waist to the hem, so revealing the dress beneath. The headwear worn was the popular French hood.

The lady on the left is wearing a Dutch-style hood, or 'cornet', with lappets. This was made of lawn, linen and white gauze or muslin with wire frames. The one-piece gown, worn over the bodice and skirt, fitted the figure at the waist then overhung the hips; the full, gathered skirt falling to the ground. The French full sleeves expanded into wide turned-back cuffs, showing the lining of quilted velvet. Broad bands or guards of velvet decorated the sleeves. A distinctive feature of the costume was the full, sheer *guimpe* or chemise which appeared through the square-shaped *décolletage*. The bodice of the gown was open from the neck to the waist.

14 English gentleman and Spanish lady, c. 1560–72

The lady is wearing a court bonnet decorated with pearls and drooping ostrich feathers. This bonnet was worn over a jewelled caul, and was known as a 'taffeta pipkin'. The bodice of the dress was corseted, coming down to a deep point in front with the bell-shaped hoop of Spanish origin. This bodice was close-fitting down to the waist, then expanded over the hips. The high-necked collar was surrounded by a medium-sized, closed-all-round ruff. The sleeves were full, hanging down almost to the hem, and worn over undersleeves of brocaded satin with lace edgings at the cuffs, forming wrist ruffs.

The gentleman wears Venetian breeches or slops, which were voluminous with looped borders in pickadils at the knees. The jerkin was tied by points, but usually fastened only at the chest and then allowed to open so as to reveal the doublet beneath. Stray points fastened the breeches to the undersurface of the doublet which had modified trunk sleeves. The high-necked doublet had a medium-sized ruff, closed all round; the band strings were tied and concealed. The doublet in this Venetian style was padded at the stomach, giving the appearance of a peascod. The hair was fairly short. Hand ruffs, made like small neck ruffs, were usually worn.

15 Young lady and gentleman, c. 1564–9

The young lady is wearing a deep-pointed bodice with a low, square neckline. Around the high neck was worn a small ruff. The short, puffed-out sleeves were worn over long, close undersleeves. The border of the neckline and down the front of the open shirt was similar to the pickadils. The headwear was the very popular 'taffeta pipkin'. The deep crown was pleated onto a head band; the brim was flat and narrow. The hat was decorated with ostrich tips and aigrettes.

The young gentleman wears a doublet with a high-standing collar and a small ruff above. The doublet was closed down the front from the top of the collar to the waist, by a row of small buttons fairly close together. A narrow belt and sling was worn around the waist, and supported a sword on the left side. The cloak with hanging sleeves was possibly made of silk brocade and was lined and edged with fur. It had a standing collar reaching down to the bottom of the trunk hose, which were paned. Panes were long thin strips of material which ran parallel and were joined to the hose at the waist and at the ends. The tailored stockings were quite plain. The pumps had rounded toes and were closed at the ankles. The bonnet was trimmed around the edge and decorated with a plume on one side. Short perfumed gloves were carried.

16 Spanish nobleman and lady, c. 1565

The lady illustrated wears a loose-bodied gown which fitted the shoulders, then hung down in stiff folds to the ground. The gown had a standing collar with rounded corners, and was tied in front. Sometimes a narrow girdle fastened the gown at the waist. The sleeves were close-fitting to the wrist and finished with a deep, turned-back cuff of lace. A reticulated caul was worn which covered the back of the head, leaving the forehead uncovered.

The gentleman wears a close-fitting, deep-waisted, sleeveless jerkin which buttoned down the front from the high collar to the waistline. The long skirt expanded over the bombasted, slashed trunk hose and reached just below the fork. The exposed sleeves of the doublet were close-fitting and finished at the wrists with ruffs which matched the short, neck ruff. The cloak was sleeveless and hung down just below the trunk hose. The tailored stockings were cut on the cross and called nether-stocks. Shoes were made in various materials such as leather, silk, brocade and velvet. The court bonnet was made in velvet or cloth and trimmed with jewelled ornaments and a small feather plume. Short, fine leather gloves with a contrasting colour at the wrists were worn. Walking sticks of wood, usually long with decorative metal knobs, were often carried.

17 Spanish princess in a farthingale, c. 1571

The illustration shows a Spanish-style gown, an overgarment for warmth and formal occasions, which was worn over the bodice and skirt. The close-bodied gown fitted the figure to the waist then extended over the hips. Fitting close to the shoulders it fell spreading outwards to the ground, leaving an inverted V-shaped opening in front from the waist to the hem. The Spanish farthingale, or verdingale, was an underskirt distended by circular hoops, each hoop increasing in circumference finally forming a wide circle at the feet, so producing a funnel shape. This farthingale skirt was gored so that it sloped stiffly outwards from the waist to the ground, making a smooth flat surface without folds, and was called a 'round kirtle'. The gown had a standing collar, tied or buttoned in front. Long sham hanging sleeves, brocaded and silk lined, fastened at just below elbow level by ribbon and jewelled points. A large opening then revealed the undersleeve of the undergarment made of batiste with lace ribbon loops. A small ruff was attached to the high collar of the chemise. The lady wore the small Mary Stuart hood-type of headdress made of lawn or similar material and trimmed with lace and jewellery. Gloves were worn, made of scented leather; and called 'sweet gloves'. A handkerchief of lawn, trimmed with lace was carried.

18 Fashionable German lady and gentleman, c. 1580

This German style worn by the lady, was a variation of the gown overgarment which was worn over the bodice and skirt. The front was open in an inverted V-shape from neck to hem. The gown was untrained, and the standing collar with rounded edges was left open. A small, closed frill was attached to the high collar of the bodice of the undergarment. Narrow, wrist frills were attached to the close-fitting, long undergarment sleeves. The reticulated caul was lined with silk and was worn covering the back of the head.

The gentleman wears a close-fitting doublet which was worn over the skirt. The body of the doublet was padded and stiffened. The collar was high at the back, curving out slightly in front. A small closed ruff was also worn. The full-padded trunk sleeves finished with a narrow hand ruff. The sleeves were slashed. The doublet was fastened by a close row of buttons from the top of the collar to the waist. The plain skirt was very short and narrow, little more than a border. The front edges were cut to form a small inverted V-shape. The trunk hose sloped outwards from the waist, and were decorated with panes – gay coloured linings drawn through gaps. The shoes were bluntly pointed, without heels. The cloak worn was hip length and had a standing collar.

19 Going to the ball – German style, c. 1580

At this period, Spanish ladies' fashions were introduced into Germany, the underdress had a long close-fitting bodice of a quilted material. The overdress fitted only at the shoulders and gradually increased in width downwards. The gown was open down the front. The sleeves were the long, tubular type of hanging sleeve joined at the elbow. The gown was decorated with broad guards or bands of braid. Cartwheel ruffs of large dimensions were now in fashion. These ruffs were made of linen, and were starched and ironed for stiffness. The headwear worn was a coif – a one-piece hat which had a seam along the top. A fan was carried.

The gentleman wears the 'copotain' type of headwear which had a conical-shaped, high crown and a narrow brim ornamented with ostrich feather tips. The bombasted doublet, pointed in the front, was fastened down the centre with a single row of buttons. The cloak, which ended just below the waist, had a turned-down collar. The trunk hose were short and pumpkin-shaped, and bombasted with padding to give fullness. The shoes were full to the ankle and were slashed in the fashionable mode.

20 Spanish lady in jewelled gown, and nobleman, c. 1590

The gentleman wears the high-necked, bombasted doublet of the Spanish style. The doublet was slashed, pinked and embroidered and had a centre fastening with buttons from the neck to the waist. The sleeves were close-fitting to the wrist, ending in small wrist ruffs. Like the doublet, the sleeves were also slashed and pinked. On the shoulders were narrow wings covering the joins of the sleeves to the doublet. The trunk hose were shaped like padded pumpkins and reached down to about mid-thigh. The stockings were tailored to individual requirements. The short, hip-length cloak was collarless, designed to fit the shoulders and flare out over the doublet. The hat was tall with a flat top and a narrow curled brim, decorated with a narrow jewelled hat band and a feather.

The lady wears the corseted bodice with a deep point. The heavy, jewel encrusted, long stomacher-front dipped to a point. Full trunk-type sleeves with large, laced wrist cuffs of the under-bodice were revealed under the huge hanging sleeves. The gown fitted the shoulders and the figure to the waist, then expanded over the hips and fell stiffly to the ground forming a large funnel shape. Above the hanging sleeves were shoulder wings. The lace ruff was both starched and wired. The brocade gown was heavily embroidered and ornamented with encrustations of jewels. A folding fan was carried.

21 Young prince and princess, c. 1614

The young lady wears the French wheel farthingale. The fully-gathered, tub-shaped skirt was worn over this farthingale structure, and fell vertically to the ground in stiff folds. The dress bodice was close fitting to the body with a low, rounded neckline, and a point at the waist. The sleeves, of the cannon type, were slightly padded, had a 'kick-up' at the shoulders and narrowed to the wrists. Here they were fastened, and then finished off with a lace turned-back cuff. The low *décolletage* had a lace border across the shoulder and ended in a V-shape at the front. Rising from either side of the *décolletage* a fan-shaped ruff spread out round the back of the head. A caul or small round hat was worn at the back of the head and a folding fan was carried.

The boy wears the longer waisted doublet which fitted close to the body. It had a narrow tabbed pointed skirt. The doublet was fastened down the front by a close row of buttons. The sleeves were plain and close-fitting, fastening at the wrists by a row of buttons, then ending with a turn-back lace cuff. A highly-decorated narrow sword belt hung around the waist. The trunk hose were attached to a tight waistband then expanded outwards and downwards. They combined two materials of velvet stripes and panne velvet with braid. The stockings were decorated just below the knees with sashes and ribbon rosettes. The shoes were round-toed, and decorated with large shoe roses.

22 English fashions, c. 1616

The lady wore a high-waisted embroidered jacket. It was an unpadded type of bodice which was close-fitting and flared from the waist in a basque, ending in a straight line around the hips. The high neckline was round, collarless, and filled in with a small neck ruff of lace. The sleeves were tight-fitting to the wrist; a broad wing covered the join between the sleeve and shoulder. An embroidered jacket of this type was often worn with loose open gowns and transparent aprons. This plate shows a heavily embroidered skirt which gathered at the waist and fell vertically to the ground; it was worn without a farthingale. The hair was brushed-up high on the forehead and temples, then laid over roll pads; the back hair was concealed by a caul.

The gentleman wears a close-fitting doublet. The doublet had a high-standing collar and was buttoned in front down to the waist. The sleeves were straight and close-fitting with wings at the shoulders and ended in turn-back lace cuffs. The neckwear consisted of a standing band made of a transparent material edged with lace. In this plate an armoured gorget surrounds the neck. The trunk hose were large and heavily padded. The stockings were tailored, and embroidered designs reached almost to the knees. The whole costume was heavily embroidered, braided and lace trimmed. The round-toed shoes tied at the front; the ties being hidden by huge roses.

23 A gentleman in armour and a fashionable gentleman, c. 1625

The gentleman on the right wears a high-waisted, loose-fitting doublet. The doublet was fastened from the high-standing collar to the waist by a close row of buttons down the front. The breast of the doublet was paned, as was the upper part of the broad projecting winged sleeves. The close-fitting lower part of the sleeves ended in a deep turn-back cuff of lace. An underpropper caused the semi-circular collar to stand up round the back of the head. The trunk hose were paned and were worn with stockings. The shoes were decorated with a ribbon tie. Over the arm was carried a draped cloak.

The military gentleman on the left wears a full suit of armour. Around his neck he wore a falling band – a wide lace collar which spread horizontally across the shoulders. The lace cuffs were turned back over the armour-covered sleeves. Across the body, from the right shoulder to the left hand side, was a broad lace-decorated baldrick. Breeches were worn stuffed into the top of the boots. The boots were fitted with spurs. From a waist belt and slings hung the sword. The armour of this period was usually described as 'cuirassier's armour'. From the waist of the breastplate to the knees were worn long tassets or thigh pieces, made up from many lames. The lower thigh armour was attached to the breastplate by straps or turning pins. *Pauldrons* and *vambraces*, armour pieces for the arms, were joined into one movable piece. The knees were protected by specially made *genouillières*, knee guards.

24 German soldier and boy, c. 1628

The German soldier wears the high-waisted doublet which was fastened from the high neck to the waist with a close row of buttons. The close-fitting sleeves of the lower arms had short turn-back cuffs; the upper arms were paned and finished with a projecting wing. The trunk hose sloped downwards and outwards in folds from a tight waist band. At mid-thigh the hose were turned in, and from this wide base came close-fitting cannions. The cannions were worn over long stockings. Shoes with low heels were worn, fastened by ribbon ties. Across the body was worn the broad baldrick, and in a leather type frog a sword was carried. A tall hat with a wide brim ornamented with feathers was worn.

The young boy wears the same style of clothes as his elders. The doublet was fastened from neck to waist with a close row of buttons down the centre. At the waist were ribbon points which attached the trunk hose to the doublet. The upper part of the broad, winged sleeves were paned, and the tight-fitting lower sleeves ended in turned-back lace cuffs. The trunk hose were closely gathered at the waist and fell in folds ending just above the knees. Large sash garters with rosettes were tied just below the knees. Open-sided shoes with ribbon ties were worn.

25 Lady in black, and boy, c. 1628

The boy wears a doublet with a deep skirt. The doublet was fastened by a row of buttons. The skirt overlapped at the sides, while the two pointed tabs at the front came edge to edge. The breast of the doublet was paned as were the upper winged sleeves and the lower closer-fitting sleeves which ended with a turn-back cuff of lace. The high neck of the doublet was concealed by the falling band collar as were the band strings of the ruff. The 'cloak bag' breeches worn by the boy were gathered at the waist and fell to just below the knees. The open-sided shoes with ribbon rosette ties were still popular.

The lady wears the new style of costume. The tight-fitting bodice to the waist was stiff and boned. It was fastened down the front and a stomacher laced across. A fan-shaped standing band collar encircled the low *décolletage* with lace strips bordering the neckline. The bodice sleeves were finished with broad splayed turned-back cuffs with vandyked lace borders. The gown was loose, fitting the shoulders and falling in spreading folds to the ground. It was open, fastening at the waist with a ribboned rosette and four narrow sashes across the stomacher. The large elbow-length sleeves of the gown were slashed and fastened with a large ribboned rosette.

26 German soldier musicians, fifer and drummer, c. 1628

The fifer on the left wears the close-fitting doublet which was long-waisted and stiffened with buckram. The skirt of tabs overlapped each other; the two front tabs coming deeper in the front and meeting edge to edge. The neckline was V-shaped, and from this emerged a *golillia* or standing band. The doublet was fastened from neck to waist with a row of close buttons. The winged sleeves were finished with a short turned-back cuff of linen. Around the body from the right shoulder to the left hip was a baldrick. The trunk hose were gathered in at the waist, falling into folds and finishing at mid-thigh. From mid-thigh to just below the knee were attached the cannions. On the outside seam of the hose was a broad decoration of braid and buttons. The shoes were decorated with large ribbon rosettes. The high-crowned hat was cocked at the front and decorated with a hat band and feathers.

The drummer wears a sleeveless jerkin which had deep-squared skirts to hip level. The jerkin was fastened from the rounded neckline to the hem with a centre row of buttons. The slashed sleeves were attached to the wings, and ended in short, turned-back cuffs. The full baggy pluderhose were gathered at the waist and fell in folds to the knees, where they finished with ribbon garters and bows on the outside of the leg. The shoes were fastened with ribbon knots.

27 Velásquez's Spanish lady, c. 1630

The lady, after a painting by Velásquez, wears the stiff, heavy but beautiful costume of this out-moded fashion. The high-necked bodice was tight-fitting; the standing collar was concealed by the unusual fox fur ruff worn in place of the more formal linen material. The sleeves were close-fitting to the wrists, slightly padded, and had a turned-back cuff of lace. The skirt followed the shape of the understructure of the Spanish farthingale and was gored at the waist making it slope stiffly outwards. It was heavily decorated with broad guards of gold braid down the centre and around the hem. The close-fitting doublet or waistcoat was similar to that of the male doublet of the earlier period, but without padding and came to a deep rounded point in front. The deep skirt of the doublet flared out from the waist over the hips and curved down to a deep rounded sweep in the front. The neckline of the doublet sloped to a V-shape in the front, and was fastened down the front by a series of large jewelled buttons. The doublet was without sleeves, but at the shoulders were broad wings also decorated with large jewelled buttons. From these wings hung immense hanging sleeves which were edged in wide guards of gold braid. Jewelled necklaces and brooches were worn, and a large handkerchief of lawn trimmed with lace was carried.

28 German Officer and lady in riding habit, c. 1630

The lady wears the high-necked pleated bodice with a closed ruff of lawn. The sleeves were straight and fairly close-fitting. The bodice sleeves had deep lawn cuffs turned back from the wrist with wide lace borders. The skirt was full and gathered; it fell in folds to the ground and was worn without a farthingale. The doublet was close-fitting to the waist, flaring out slightly with the aid of gussets. The 'cavalier' type hat had a moderately high crown with a wide brim. The hat was worn over a coif.

The military gentleman wore the leather jerkin. The jerkin had a turned-down collar and fastened down the centre with a close row of buttons from neck to hem-line. The front seams of the sleeves were left open to reveal the chemise sleeves beneath. They finished with turned-back cuffs of lawn which were concealed by leather gauntlet gloves. Over this was a broad laced falling band which spread from shoulder to shoulder. Across the body was slung the broad leather shoulder belt which supported the sword. Around the waist was encircled a broad silk baldrick tied with a large bow at the side. The breeches were the full oval type and fastened below the knees. Also worn were high boot hose which were folded over leather boots. A 'cavalier' hat was worn, similar to that worn by the lady.

29 Lady and gentleman going to a wedding, c. 1630

The lady is wearing a basqued bodice, which was tabbed, similar to the doublet of the male dress. The *décolletage* was cut low and round in front. A narrow ribbon sash encircled the waistline and finished in a large bow in front. The sleeves of the bodice were ballooned and paned, both above and below the elbows. At the wrists the sleeves were gathered in by draw-strings and ended in large hand ruffs. The fitted bodice gown was joined to a full gathered skirt.

The gentleman depicts the advent of the cavalier fashion; the jerkin or waistcoat replacing the doublet. The sleeves were open at the seam revealing the full sleeves of the chemise or shirt. The neckline of the jerkin was hidden by the large falling band which sloped down and spread from shoulder to shoulder and was tied with band strings which were allowed to hang down. The moderately full, long-legged breeches fell to just below the knees and fastened with ribbon loops. The breeches were decorated down the outside seams and halfway down the front with brandenburgs. Short leather boots with tops of soft leather were ornamented with 'butterfly' spur leathers. The large 'cavalier' type hat, slightly cocked on one side, was trimmed with a hat band and feathers.

30 Lady and gentleman in court dress, c. 1630

The lady is wearing a tight-fitting bodice with a stomacher coming to a deep point in the front. The stomacher was stiffened and boned and fastened down the front by a row of close set buttons. The bodice had a low *décolletage* edged with lace strips. A spreading fan collar surrounded the neck. Above the wrists the sleeves were pulled in by a running draw-string, then finished off with a turned-back cuff. The gown had a fitted bodice joined to a full gathered skirt and was open down the front. The neckline was low on the shoulders. The straight sleeves, which were open down the front seam, were tied by a ribbon bow at the bend of the elbow. Around the waist was worn a narrow ribbon cord.

For the male, the doublet was now high-waisted, not quite so close-fitting, and was almost without stiffening. The tabs, or skirts, were more imposing than previously. The two front tabs were deeply pointed in front, meeting edge to edge. Surrounding the stiff high neck was a stand-fall ruff which completely concealed the neck-line. The doublet was paned at the chest front and back, revealing the full linen or silk shirt beneath. The winged sleeves were wide and paned to the elbow, then close-fitting to the wrists. Decorative gauntlet gloves concealed the turned-back lace cuffs. Long-legged breeches were full to the knee, where they were fringed with ribbon loops. The soft leather boots had their tops turned down to reveal the silk stockings.

31 Cavalier officer and lady, c. 1630

The French style *décolletage* was trimmed with a lace collar and cut in the vandyke style. The bodice was high-waisted. The sleeves were short and very full to just above the elbows, then drawn in loosely to allow the full frill of the chemise to emerge at elbow length. The closed full skirt was gathered at the waist, then allowed to fall naturally in folds to the ground. The hair was decorated with jewels.

The cavalier gentleman wears a sleeveless buff coat often called a leather jerkin. This coat was fairly close-fitting, high-waisted and had a deep skirt reaching down to just below hip length. The rounded neckline was without a collar, this being concealed by a falling band type collar. This collar was made of point lace. The coat fastened from the neck to the waist by a close row of buttons and loops. A sleeve of soft material was sewn on under the narrow welt wing. The sleeves ended with a point lace similar to the collar. The loose breeches reached to the knees and were tied with ribbon garters. The boot-hose had lace tops which showed above the high soft leather boots. Encircling the waist was a wide silk baldrick sash tied in a huge bow on the left hip. The sword was carried from a waist belt and frog. The 'cavalier' style hat had a moderately high crown, a very broad brim and was usually worn in a cocked position.

32 Musketeer and country girl in pattens, c. 1633

The country woman's clothes were an attempt to keep up with the trend of the day. The bodice was close-fitting and high-waisted with a basque. The bodice was open in front and pulled together by means of lacing. A stomacher was pinned to the front. A plain neckerchief – a large square of fine material folded diagonally – was worn over the shoulders like a shawl and fastened in the front at the throat. The full skirt was gathered at the waist and fell in folds to the ground. A coif or day cap was worn over the hair and round the back of the neck. Pattens were worn; these were wooden-soled overshoes raised up on iron rings. They were secured by straps and worn with ordinary shoes.

The musketeer wears the hip-length sleeveless buff jerkin. Close-fitting sleeves were sewn under the wings on the shoulders; the cuffs of these sleeves were hidden under short gauntlet gloves. The full pluderhose type breeches fell in irregular folds to just below the knees. The outside seams of the trunk hose were decorated with buttons and loops. High shoes were worn. A bandolier, with flasks, bullet bag, charges, and keys or 'spanners' for the matchlock gun, was carried from the left shoulder across the body to the right hip. This musketeer carried a wooden rest to support the heavy matchlock barrel. He also carried a coil of slow-burning 'match'. A high-crowned hat with a wide brim decorated with feathers.

33 Nobleman and boy in hunting attire, c. 1635

The nobleman is wearing a leather jerkin which was close-fitting to the body, had a high waistline and a deep skirt overlapping in front. The jerkin was without a collar and came to a small V-shape at the neck. This was filled in by a falling band collar of lawn. The fastening of the jerkin was from the neck to the waist by close lacing. A narrow belt encircled the waist. The loose winged sleeves were worn hanging. Close-fitting sleeves of a softer material were attached under the wings.

The trunk hose were in the 'cloak bag' breeches style, gathered at the waist and closed just below the knees. High boots of soft leather were worn as was a tall-crowned hat of soft leather or material.

The little boy dressed in similar clothes to the adults. The leather jerkin was loose-fitting. There was no collar but the neckline opened in a small V-shape and was filled by a falling band collar of lawn, usually lace decorated. Attached to the wings were the tubular hanging sleeves of leather and softer material sleeves, close-fitting to the wrists. The breeches were fastened just below the knees. Long soft leather boots were worn. A low-crowned hat with a peak was worn at a slight angle. Plain gauntlet gloves of soft leather were worn in the adult style, extended well above the wrists.

34 English earl and lady in court dress, c. 1635

The bodice of the new styles for women was high-waisted, worn with a basque. The bodice had a low *décolletage* with a broad lace-edged bertha – a wide lingerie collar which came from the edges of the *décolletage* over the shoulders and around the back. A narrow ribbon sash followed the waistline and tied in a spreading bow. The sleeves were full to the elbow with close pleats at the shoulders and at the elbows. At the elbows they were gathered on to a band, or sometimes drawn with a running string, but left loose enough to allow the frilled undersleeve to come through. The closed skirt was loosely gathered at the waist and fell to the ground in folds.

The man wears the embroidered, close-fitting doublet which was high-waisted and had deep-skirted tabs. The doublet had a standing collar which was concealed by a falling band collar of lawn and lace vandykes. The fastening was from neck to waist by a centre row of buttons. The sleeves had a longitudinal slash on the front seam which revealed the full lawn chemise sleeve below. The long-legged breeches ended just below the knees. Down the outside seam of the breeches were decorations of loops of braid and buttons. Silk stockings were worn with open-sided, low-heeled shoes. A large cloak was draped around the figure.

35 Countess and child, c. 1640

The lady is wearing a high-waisted bodice which was close-fitting and stiffened with whalebone. The *décolletage* was cut low in the front and high at the back. It encircled the bust and partially bared the shoulders. The lace of the chemise bordered the *décolletage*. The fastening of the bodice was at the back. The sleeves were full with a wide lace-edged opening just above the elbow. The just below elbow-length sleeves of the chemise with their frilly ends emerged below the bodice sleeve. The full skirt was gathered at the waist and hung in loose folds to the ground. A narrow jewelled belt encircled the waistline.

The little girl was dressed in a similar style. The bodice was high-waisted and close-fitting, being stiffened with whalebone. The square *décolletage* was cut low in the front and high at the back. The sleeves were full, tapering down to just above the wrists and ended with a deep turned-back cuff of lace which was vandyked. The skirt was gathered at the waist and allowed to fall in vertical folds to the ground. The hair was in the same style as that of the lady, and decorated with ribbon. Jewellery was worn by children in much the same way as adults.

36 Merchants' wives, English and Dutch fashions, c. 1640

The English lady on the left wore the close-fitting bodice which was high-waisted with a low *décolletage* and a chemisette fill-in. The neck was encircled with a large ruff, oval in shape. The sleeves were full and puffed to the wrist in the 'bishop' style, and finished with a deep turn-back cuff with a lace edge.

The 'sugarloaf' hat had a high crown which sloped to a narrow flat top. The hat was worn over a white coif or under-cap. A medium-sized fur muff was carried by the more wealthy merchants' wives.

The Dutch fashion for middle-class ladies favoured the basqued bodice. The short sleeves of the bodice were castellated and just covered the shoulder joins. The bodice was paned and fastened down the centre of the front. The undersleeves were close-fitting and long to the wrist, ending in a turn-back cuff which was edged with lace and vandyked. Around the high neckline of the bodice was a closed cartwheel ruff worn mainly by married women. The closed skirt was gathered loosely at the waist, falling in irregular folds to the ground. A plain white apron was worn. A wired day-cap was worn which was placed over the back of the head and around the back of the neck. The cap was not tied under the chin, but was attached to the hair by a pinner.

37 Lady in 'chaperone' and mask, with nobleman, c. 1640

The lady is wearing an informal out-of-doors costume. On her head she wore the 'chaperone', a soft hood which covered the head and framed the face. Over her dress she wore the long, voluminous 'cassock' or overcoat. Around the neckline was a small, round, turned-down collar, and the coat was fastened from the neck to the hem with buttons down the centre of the front. On her face the lady wore a half-mask ending just below the nose. Masks were very popular and were mainly worn by ladies. A large feather fan with a decorative handle and a mirror was carried on a ribbon cord attached to a waist girdle. A fairly large fur muff was carried either in the hand or on a cord from around the neck.

The man wears the close-fitting, high-waisted doublet. Deep skirts flared out to mid-thigh, overlapping slightly in the front. The breast front and the back had vertical panes down to waist level. From the small projecting wings hung the sleeves which were full and paned from the shoulder to the elbow, then close-fitting to the wrist. The neck was encircled by a broad falling band of vandyke-edged lace. The long-legged breeches, or Spanish hose, were worn with high boots of fine leather, topped with the fine lace turn-down of the boat hose.

38 Country gentleman and his wife, c. 1640

The lady is dressed in the high-waisted, basqued bodice. The basque, like the male doublet, was tabbed; the tabs being squared and deep. The plain stomacher was pinned to the front borders. The neckline formed a low *décolletage* in front but was cut higher at the back in a square shape. The broad bertha of deeply bordered lace was worn with a large, square, lace-edged neckerchief. The 'coat' sleeve was double; the upper sleeve finishing at the elbow, the lower sleeve close-fitting and ending at the wrist with a lace turned-back cuff. The skirt was gathered loosely at the waist, and fell in irregular vertical folds to the ground.

The gentleman wears the ornamental leather jerkin or buff coat. The coat was close-fitting with a high waistline and a deep skirt reaching hip length; it was slit at the back, and quite often at the sides. Hanging from the coat wings were close-fitting sleeves, usually of a soft cloth material, often trimmed with lace or braid in longitudinal stripes. The neckline of the coat was concealed under a broad lace falling-band collar. The coat was decorated overall in stripes of braid and buttons. The full breeches, or Spanish hose as they were known, stretched from the waist to below the knee. The breeches, like the jerkin, were decorated with braid and lace.

39 Children of a royal family, c. 1641

The young girl wears a short-waisted bodice fastened at the front, either by lacing or clasps. The bodice had a low square *décolletage* in front with a higher cut square back. A deep, lace-bordered collar, surrounded the *décolletage* and ended just in front of the shoulders. The coat sleeve was double; the over-sleeve ending at the elbow, the sleeve beneath coming lower and ending in a turned-back lace cuff. The skirt was gathered at the waist and fell in folds to the ground. A narrow ribbon girdle followed the contours of the waistline and was tied into a spreading bow on the side.

The boy wears the high-waisted, loose-fitting doublet. The neckline had a short standing collar. The doublet was fastened from neck to waist by a row of close buttons. It was paned down the breast and at the back, matching the sleeve fashion. The neck was encircled with a broad lace falling band. The long-legged breeches, pleated into a waist band fell to just below the knees, where they were closed by a ribbon sash. Silk stockings were worn. The shoes, with side openings, had large ribbon bows as fastenings. A wide-brimmed hat with a moderately high conical crown and a decorative hat band was fashionable. The French type of cloak was worn draped over the body.

40 Ladies in summer fashions, c. 1643

The lady on the left is wearing a spring or early summer fashion. The high-waisted bodice was made with a basque. The bodice was fastened at the back by a series of clasps; it was worn without a stomacher but had a chemisette fill-in which was laced across. The neck had a low *décolletage* in front but was cut much higher at the back. The neck was encircled with a bertha type collar. The bodice had a turned-down narrow lace edging in front. Over this was a lace-edged square neckerchief which was folded corner-wise. The sleeves were in two parts; an oversleeve or 'coat' sleeve and an undersleeve which came a little lower than elbow length and ended with a turned-back cuff finished with lace. The moderately full skirt was gathered in at the waist and fell in folds to the ground.

The lady on the right is dressed in a high summer fashion of the period. The bodice was high-waisted with a basque. The neckline of the low *décolletage* was encircled by a broad bertha. The sleeves consisted of an epaulette, an oversleeve, and an undersleeve. Long elbow-length gloves were close-fitting and always worn with short-sleeved bodices. The full skirt was frequently bunched up in a casual way to show the full elegance and beautiful material of the underskirt. Over the head and face was a plain gauze veil.

41 English lady in furs and mask, and a Dutch lady, c. 1643

The English lady on the left wears a bodice with the low *décolletage* covered by both a broad bertha collar and a neckerchief. The sleeves were reasonably close-fitting, ending just above the wrists with a turned-back cuff, often open behind. The skirt was moderately full, gathered at the waist and allowed to fall to the ground in irregular vertical folds. Both the skirt and the underskirt were sometimes bunched up in a variety of ways, exposing the more delicate silken fabric of the under-petticoat. The hood, or 'chaperone', was of a soft material, often silken lined and worn only for outdoors. A deep fur stole was worn around the neck and shoulders, and a matching large fur muff was carried in the hand. On the face is shown a half-mask of black velvet covering the upper part of the face only.

The lady on the right wears a high-waisted bodice with a deep V-shaped stomacher. The neckline trimming was the closed cartwheel ruff which tilted up at the back and down in the front. The heavy full skirt was gathered into the waist and fell in folds to the ground. It was hitched up to about knee level and revealed the underskirt. The close-fitting sleeves came to just below elbow length and ended with deep turned-back lace cuffs.

42 Autumnal fashions of a lady and child, c. 1650

The girl's bodice was short waisted, with the neck forming a low *décolletage* in front, cut in the off-the-shoulder style, and encircled by a bertha collar. The sleeve was full and ended just below the elbow. The front seam was open revealing the brocaded lining beneath. The full skirt was gathered at the waist and fell in folds to the ground. Over the bodice was worn an apron with a bib. A laced day-cap was worn and arranged to frame the face.

The lady is wearing an autumn fashion, as depicted by Wenceslaus Hollar. The bodice was tight-fitting to the waist, coming to a slight point in front. The *décolletage* was low and cut horizontally, it was draped by a broad lace bertha and edged in the front by a frill of lace. A large square neckerchief, with a broad border of lace, was worn over the shoulders and *décolletage*, and fastened at the throat by a brooch. A full sleeve fell to the elbow and finished in a deep turned-back cuff of lace. Close-fitting elbow-length gloves were worn. The moderately full skirt was gathered in at the waist, often slightly trained, and fell in folds to the ground. Over the front of the skirt was an elegant white linen apron with a lace border. Over the head was a soft hood or 'chaperone'.

43 A young Spanish princess, c. 1659

The young lady wears the same basic costume that had been fashionable for almost fifty years. The close-fitting bodice, moderately long-fronted, was joined to the stiff basque of the Spanish farthingale, which tilted down in the front and up at the back. The low, round neckline, horizontal and boat shaped, was encircled with a deep bertha collar. This low *décolletage* exposed the shoulders and the back, but came high over the bust. In the centre of the front of the bertha was a large ribboned rosette, fastened on with a jewelled brooch. The sleeves were full to the elbow, then gathered onto a band which was loose enough to permit the full frilled sleeve of the chemise to come through, and end at the wrist with a turned-back lace cuff. The sleeves were paned, revealing the sleeves of the chemise. The farthingale structure, concealed by the stiff basque, was now made of oval-shaped hoops, being flattish in the front and back, but very wide at the sides. It expanded abruptly out from the waist and continued down to the ground, the bottom hoop being as wide as the height of the person wearing the costume. The skirt fitted over the structure and fell to the ground in rather stiff folds. The hairstyle always followed the silhouette of the dress itself. It was decorated with hanging plumes.

44 Dutch nobleman and his wife, c. 1660

The lady wore the close-fitting busked and boned bodice. The *décolletage* was cut low, horizontally surrounding the bust and sloping off the shoulders; the neckline was edged with the lace of the chemise. The deep broad lace bertha was boat-shaped and encircled the *décolletage*. The sleeve was full and moderately balloon-shaped. The full skirt was gathered into small pleats at the waist, then allowed to fall to the ground in vertical folds. It was often slightly trained. The front was open to reveal the underskirt or petticoat, usually of a contrasting material, sometimes a little shorter than the overskirt.

The gentleman of fashion continued to wear the short unstiffened doublet. Its skirts were merely a narrow tabbed edging under which were trimmings of ribbon loops. The sleeves were full with the front seam slit. The high stiff neck-band was concealed by a falling band which was deep and shaped like a bib; the two front edges meeting edge to edge. The collar was square-ended and spread from shoulder to shoulder. The knee-length open breeches were decorated with ribbon loops on the lower part of the outside seam. Stirrup hose had large tops which were turned down and spread out below the knee.

45 Dutch gentleman in petticoat breeches with lady, c. 1665

This fashionable Dutch gentleman of *c.* 1665 wearing the petticoat breeches costume shows this extreme fashion at its best. He wore the short skimpy doublet. It had a stiff standing collar and buttoned down the centre front with a row of close buttons. The neck was encircled by a falling band which stretched from shoulder to shoulder, a large bib. The sleeves, with the front seam slit, finished just below the elbows. The petticoat breeches known as pantaloons, or 'rhinegraves', had very large wide legs pleated on to a waist band, then falling to the knee in heavy vertical folds. Stockings were worn, and over these a pair of stirrup hose which had a large decorative top. Shoes were square-toed, open-sided and had high square heels. The full cloak, without sleeves was worn over both shoulders. The tall 'sugar-loaf' hat was the most popular, the crown being conical in shape, narrowing to a flat top.

This Dutch lady wears a silk or satin costume with the close fitting bodice coming to a deep point in front. The *décolletage* was low cut and encircled by a large velvet collar. The full, baggy sleeves were drawn in at the elbows from which emerged the full sleeves of the chemise with frill. The full skirt was closely gathered into small pleats at the waist and fell in irregular folds.

46 Fashionable lady in evening dress, c. 1668

The female costume of this period was quite simple in contrast to the fashions of the males with their absurd petticoat breeches costume. The feminine gown had a close-fitting, boned bodice which, because of the long waist, dipped to a deep point in front, creating a slimmer look. The bodice was worn with a close-fitting corset which was high under the arms and over the bosom; both corset and bodice were laced at the back. The neckline was low cut in a rounded shape which encircled the *décolletage* and bared the shoulders. The *décolletage* was edged by the lace of the chemisette. The sleeves were full to the elbow, and left open to reveal the full frilled sleeves of the chemisette. The full skirt was gathered in pleats at the waist and hung in folds to the ground. It was usually open in front and caught up over an underskirt or petticoat. A train was present, both on the overskirt and on the underskirt. Shawls or scarves were very common and were often worn with a low *décolletage*. The hairstyle was called a *coiffure à la ninon*. The sides were cut fairly short or pushed back off the face, with curls, called *confidants*, bunched on each side, then falling to the shoulders in ringlets. Lace and ribbon bands and bows decorated the hair.

1670-1760

47 Officer in 'bucket boots', with a lady, c. 1675

Tight lacing became the main feature of female costume in Europe at this time. The bodice sloped to a deep point in front. The low *décolletage* was cut more or less horizontally. A bertha collar, sometimes called a 'falling whisk', completely enveloped the low neckline. Short tabs were often seen encircling the deep-pointed waistline and expanding over the hips. The short sleeve finished just above the elbow and was joined to the sloping shoulders of the bodice. The frilled, full sleeve of the chemise fell from the outer sleeve to just below elbow level. The full open skirt was gathered at the waist in small pleats, then allowed to fall to the ground in loose folds. The open front revealed the petticoat of silks and satins.

This French officer *c.* 1675, wears a slightly waisted *justaucorps*. The *justaucorps* was made of heavy cloth and decorated with a close row of buttons and button-holes. The pockets were placed low in the front in a vertical design while the sleeves were straight and close-fitting. Around the neck was a cravat. From the right shoulder hung a broad leather baldrick from which hung the sword at the left hip. Full wide breeches fell to the knees and large, high military boots were worn. Wigs were becoming very fashionable with hair shoulder length. The hat had a wide cocked brim.

48 French farmer and milkmaid in country costume, c. 1678

The French farmer wore the vest and *justaucorps* which hung to just above the knees. The coat was fastened from the neckline to the waist by a close row of buttons. The pockets were set low and horizontally and had button and button-hole decoration. The sleeves were just below elbow length with deep turned-back cuffs from which emerged the full shirt sleeves. The breeches, were wide and skirt-like; the large legs were pleated onto a waistband and fell to just below the knees. The stockings were of the woollen variety. The shoes were square-toed. The moderately high crown of the hat was indented and attached to a fairly wide, flat brim.

The French country girl's bodice was long-waisted, close-fitting and boned, and came to a deep point in front. The *décolletage* was low cut, but was completely covered by a linen chemise with a neck frill. The full-length sleeves ended in turned-back cuffs. The skirt was gathered at the waist and hung in full folds to the ground, but contrary to the French law at that time, the young lady had hitched up her skirt all round, *à la retroussée*, exposing the petticoat. Covering the back of the head was a 'cornet', a coif style with long lappets or ear pieces which often fell behind the shoulders.

49 Officer and his lady, c. 1678

The bodice of the lady's costume was long and close-fitting. The low *décolletage* was encircled with lace frills. The straight sleeves were elbow length and finished with lace ruffles. Long elbow-length, close-fitting gloves made of silk or fine leather were worn for all formal dress. The skirt was full and closely gathered in small pleats at the waist, then hung to the ground. The headdress was the 'cornet' – a lawn cap which had a standing frill in front and long lappets falling behind the shoulders, or tied in front under the chin.

The back view of the officer of *c.* 1678 shows the long body of the *justaucorps*. The coat was collarless and fastened down the front with buttons and fancy button-holes. The sleeves were close-fitting to the elbows, then widened slightly, ending in a turned-back cuff. Across the body from the right shoulder to the left hip was a long wide ornate baldrick which supported the sword. This was also decorated with ribbon loops, known as a 'sword knot'. Around the waist was tied a silken sash with fringed ends. Wide breeches reaching to just below the knees were very popular. Square-toed shoes, which fastened with a buckle and strap, were worn; they had large tongues over the instep. Wigs were worn by all fashionable gentlemen. The wide brim of the felt hat was cocked high in front.

50 French officer in 'bloomer' style with lady, c. 1682

The lady's tight-fitting, small-waisted bodice of the gown was joined to a full gathered skirt which was also trained. The *décolletage* formed round the back of the neck was either round or square. The sleeves were short and straight, ending just above the elbow; they were turned and fastened just below the shoulder with a button and loop. From under these sleeves emerged the full chemise sleeves. The full skirt hung to the ground and the trained overskirt was hitched up behind and at the sides. Over the head was a 'headkerchief' which fastened under the chin. Walking canes and long handled parasols called 'umbrelloes' were carried.

The French officer wore the 'bloomer' style fashion. The coat was slightly waisted, with a short flared skirt falling to just below hip level. The sleeves were close-fitting to just below elbow length. Around the neck was a linen cravat with a lace border. Across the body was the wide baldrick which supported the sword. The 'bloomer' breeches were fastened below the knee with ribbon ties and decorated with bunches of ribbon loops. The waist was also decorated with ribbon loops. The square-toed shoes were fastened with straps, large square buckles and limp bunches of ribbon loops. The shoes were usually black leather with red heels. The large, low-crowned hat had a very wide brim which was usually cocked on one side. Gauntlet gloves were worn, often embroidered or trimmed with fur. Large fur muffs, a French fashion, were carried, suspended on a ribbon round the neck.

51 Fashionable gentleman and a peasant girl, c. 1684

The French gentleman wore his coat just above knee length. The coat was collarless and fastened from neck to hem. The sleeves were now longer, finishing nearer the wrist. Down the front, around the skirt and around the cuffs, the coat was heavily decorated with buttons and braid. The neck was enclosed with a linen cravat. The coat was worn without a waistcoat and revealed the full shirt beneath. The 'bloomer' leg breeches were gathered onto a band just below the knee, with the fullness expanding slightly over the ribbon loop gartering. The shoes tapered to a square-toe, and fastened over the high tongue with a strap and buckle. The wigs continued to be large, usually longer on the left side. The low-crowned hat was called a 'boater shape' hat. Large gauntlet gloves were fringed with lace and fur. Walking sticks were carried.

The woman's costume was without frills. The bodice was close-fitting and open to the waist in front but was filled in with a laced 'corset'. The skirt was gathered onto the bodice in close pleats and fell to ankle length. Full sleeves ended at the elbows and had turned or rolled-up cuffs without frills or ruffles. Also of coarse linen was the large apron. The leather shoes tapered to a square toe and were fastened with a narrow ribbon. The head was covered with a headkerchief wrapped around the hair.

52 Palace guard officer and lady with a 'fontange', (headdress), c. 1693

For the lady, the bodice was close-fitting and joined to a gathered and trained full skirt. The gap in front was filled-in with a stomacher which came to a point in the front just below waist level. The straight sleeve ended just above the elbow with a turned-up cuff. The frilled ruffle of the chemise dropped from the sleeve of the bodice. The trained skirt was taken back and hitched up, often over a bustle, *cul de Paris*. The exposed underskirt or petticoat was trimmed at hip level with a reversed flounce, fringed with lace. The hem was embroidered with a lace edging. High, close-fitting elbow-length gloves were worn. The hairstyle was called the 'fontange' coiffure. Patches, or 'mouches' were worn on the face as a mark of beauty.

The male wore the mixed fashions of the day. The coat was close-fitting down to the waist, the skirts flaring out to mid-thigh. The coat was closed to chest level only, then worn open to reveal the chemise shirt beneath. The pockets were set very low. The sleeves were tight-fitting, ending near the wrist with a turned-up cuff. From this cuff emerged a deep ruffle, decorated with ribbon bows. The full breeches ended just below the knees and were tied with ribbon garters with hanging loops. The shoes tapered to a square toe. The wig of long ringlets fell over the shoulders. The large brimmed hat with the low crown was decorated around the edge with braid and ostrich feathers.

53 Gentleman of quality and a fashionable lady, c. 1694

The close-fitting bodice with the full, gathered and trained skirt worn open in front continued in female fashion. The sleeves remained short to the elbow with a turned-up cuff and deep ruffles emerging below. The bustle effect became very apparent. Around the neck was worn a 'pallatine' or tippet of sable; this was a scarf of fur tied loosely around the neck with the two ends dangling down either side. A medium-sized muff of matching fur was carried. The hair was parted in the centre and wired up above the forehead forming two high peaks on either side, then fashioned onto the 'fontange' headdress. The fontage was tall and narrow, with one tier built over another, reaching a considerable height. It was shaped like a half-closed fan tilting slightly forward. The two long linen streamers were often pinned up to the crown.

Men's coats became slightly more waisted with flared skirts coming down to knee length. They fastened from the still collarless neckline to the hem with buttons, but were now left completely open. Around the neck was the fashionable Steinkirk cravat. The waistcoat, similar to the coat, was close-fitting and ended just above the knee. Close-fitting, knee-length breeches, almost concealed by the coat, were fastened below the knee with either buttons or buckles. The wide-brimmed hat edged with braid and decorated with feathers, was worn cocked to one side or in whatever manner fashion decreed.

54 Nobleman and his son, c. 1695

The closing years of the seventeenth century brought no essential changes in fashionable male dress. The coats were close-fitting to the waist with flaring skirts in various lengths. The pleated side vents and the back slit still dominated the coat. The coat was usually collarless and fastened down the front with buttons. Usually all buttons, or those from the neck to the waist or from the chest to the hem, were left unfastened, according to the fashionable whim of the time. The sleeves were close-fitting with large or medium-sized turned-back cuffs. Cravats were of linen with lace borders. The breeches were, in most cases, plain and close-fitting. They were fastened at the knee by buttons or buckles. Cloaks, if worn, were hung over both shoulders. The essential items of fashion were the large wigs of tight curls evenly arranged and framing the face. Shoes did not alter.

The boy was dressed in the same style and fashion as his elders. The only difference was that he wore his own hair; children never took up the fashionable adornment of wigs.

55 Officer with snuffbox and lady, c. 1698

The French officer wore the close-fitting coat and the flaring skirts which ended just above the knees. The fastening was from the round collarless neck to the hem of the coat with a close row of buttons and braided button-holes. The sleeves were close-fitting, ending in a turned-back cuff from which emerged the sleeve of the shirt with ribbon bows. The neck was covered by a cravat and a ribbon bow. Over the shoulder was a broad baldrick from which hung the sword with the ribbon loops or knots. Encircling the waist was a fringed silk sash. The breeches ended just above the knees. The long ringlet wig, which hung over the shoulders and back, was ornamented with ribbon bows. The wide-brimmed hat was feather trimmed and decorated with ribbon bows.

The lady's gown was the height of fashion at this time. The bodice, open in front to the waist, was filled in either by a stomacher or an embroidered 'corset'. The bodice came up to the neck at the back and was edged in folds of muslin. The 'fill-in' was of soft lawn and it completely covered the *décolletage*. The gathered, trained skirt was joined to the bodice and hitched up towards the bustle-like back. The exposed petticoat was heavily embroidered around the hips and at the hem with heavy ruffles or 'furbelows'.

56 French General with lady in riding habit, c. 1704

The French officer wore the close-fitting coat reaching just below the knees. The skirt vents remained, as in the past decades, the open slit at the back and two pleated side vents reaching to hip level. The neck of the coat was low and collarless. The coat was fastened from neck to hem by dome-shaped, medium-sized buttons surrounded by heavy ornamentation or 'frogging'. The sleeves were close-fitting and ended with deep, round turned-back cuffs. The frilled shirt sleeve cuffs emerged from below the coat sleeve cuff. The waistcoat was embroidered and was open to just below the chest to reveal the Steinkirk neckwear. The knee breeches were fastened just below the knee with a kneeband. A wide silk sash encircled the waist. The full-bottomed French wig remained in fashion with a mass of curls framing the face, then falling down the back and over the shoulders. The cocked hat, or tricorne, was worn.

The lady's riding attire had a back slit and two pleated side vents in the jacket. The jacket was close-fitting to the waist, then the skirts flared out to just below knee level. The sleeves were close-fitting and ended with a turned-back cuff, from which emerged the full sleeve of the chemise. Around the neck was the Steinkirk neckwear. The petticoat was long, full, and often trained. The wig rose up in two points on each side of a central parting.

57 Gentleman in morning gown, c. 1712

Morning gowns of Oriental and Asian design were worn by men as négligées. The morning gown was not unlike the dressing gown worn by men today. It was a loose gown which fell to just below the knee, and had a roll collar and a wrap-over front. The full sleeves were turned or rolled back from the wrists, with the frilled sleeves of the shirt emerging below. The gown often tied at the waist with a sash. It came in a variety of materials such as damask, brocade, satin, chintz and silk. Although in most cases the gown was worn with a nightcap, it was not uncommon for a gentleman to remove his coat and vest and then don his morning gown for ease. The large full-bottomed wig was still popular and was divided into three parts; one down the back and the other two down either shoulder. Powder was used to clean the wigs, and being light brown or whitish grey in colour, tended to give a greying effect. Perfume was also used on wigs. To accommodate these hot and cumbersome wig styles, the hair was either cut very short or completely shaven off.

58 Officer and his lady, c. 1720

The lady is wearing a separate bodice and skirt. The bodice of the jacket, doublet or *casaquin* was close-fitting to the waist where the skirt was basqued and flared out over the petticoat. The bodice fastened down the front to the waist by hooks and eyes, concealed by a fly closure. The sleeves were close-fitting and ended just below the elbow; the frilled cuff of the chemise emerged below. The petticoat was untrimmed and worn over dome-shaped hoops.

The military officer is dressed in a low-necked collarless coat which buttoned from neck to hem but was always worn open. The sleeves were close-fitting and ended with a deep turned-back cuff, from which the frilled cuff of the shirt sleeve emerged. The waistcoat, decorated similarly to the coat, was worn open at the chest to reveal the cravat. A silken sash encircled the waistcoat. Close-fitting knee breeches were enclosed under heavy jackboots which reached above the knees with slightly flaring 'bucket tops'. The boots were square-toed and worn with spur leathers and metal spurs with star rowels. The campaign wig was worn; this framed the face from a central parting and fell on to both shoulders. Plain leather gauntlet gloves were carried. The three cornered hat with the low crown was worn.

59 Lady in riding habit wearing a Steinkirk cravat, c. 1720

As horse-riding was an essential part of life, and also a fashionable sport, women who followed this pursuit wore the more practical styles of their day. The female riding habit, apart from the petticoat, was therefore a copy of the male fashion. The coat followed the mode of the collarless coat for men. It had a back slit and two pleated side vents which gave the stand-out effect. The coat had fastenings from neck to hem, but was left open revealing the close-fitting waistcoat, which was fastened at the waist only. The fastening of both the coat and the waistcoat followed the male fashion of being buttoned left over right. The top opening showed the popular neckwear, namely the Steinkirk cravat. The opening from the waist down showed the deep inverted flounce of the petticoat at about mid-thigh level. The petticoat was full and fell to about ankle depth. The hem was surrounded by a deep lace border. The hair was covered by a full wig, again following the male fashion. This framed the face and fell down the back and on either side. The male tricorne, or three cornered hat, was worn or carried. A tasselled riding crop was carried, and short gauntlet gloves of the riding type were worn.

60 Fashionable gentlemen of quality, c. 1725

The two gentlemen are wearing similar outfits. The coat was close-fitting and waisted with the fully flared skirt reaching to just below the knees. The back centre slit and the two side slits continued to be worn. The coat was without a collar and was cut rather low in front. It fastened with buttons and button-holes from the neck to waist level. The sleeves were close-fitting with deep cuffs ending well above the wrist. The gentleman standing wore the round cuff; the gentleman sitting wore the 'boot' cuff. The vest, or waistcoat, closely resembled the coat. It was close-fitting to the waist and had flaring skirts stiffened with buckram. The fastening was with buttons and button-holes from neck to hem. It fastened by one or two buttons at the neck and was then open to the waist, revealing the ruffles at the neck. It was again fastened at the waist, by one or two buttons, and then unfastened to the hem. The breeches were gathered onto a waist band with the leg narrowing downwards, finishing just below the knee in a kneeband over the stocking. The shoes had blocked square toes with square high heels. The uppers of the shoes finished in square tongues which were high in front of the ankle. The sides were closed and the fastening was by straps and buckles over the instep.

61 Officer in armoured breastplate with lady, c. 1727

The lady depicted wears a closed robe with a bodice that had short robings and a stomacher front, similar to that worn with the open gown, but with a front fall fastening to the petticoat. A handkerchief or modesty piece and tucker was always worn to cover the low *décolletage*. The skirt was made with a short fall at the front pleated onto a waist-band. This gown was worn with dome-shaped hoops, often called 'pocket hoops' which were for day use only. The sleeves finished at the elbows with frilled cuffs appearing below. The undress mop cap was worn with the border encircling the face.

The military gentleman wore the fashionable coat, vest and breeches of the day. Over this he wore the sign of his profession – the last vestige of a by-gone age – armour. The chest and back were covered with the *cuirass* and *epaulières*; the upper arms were covered with *brassarts*. Over the front of the thighs were *gardefaude*, *tuille* or tassets. A baldrick and waist sash were worn, denoting the high rank of the officer. High 'bucket top' boots were worn with spur leathers and spurs. The campaign wig was surmounted by the cocked hat of the military style, called a 'kevenhuller hat'. The brim was bound in open-work lace and edged with a feather fringe.

62 Lady wearing a mantua, and gentleman in redingote, c. 1729

The lady shows the back view of the 'mantua' style gown. This was basically an open robe, but worn with a petticoat. The close-fitting, long-waisted bodice was unboned and shaped to the underlying corset. The corset, replacing the stomacher, could have been embroidered or plain in front. The close-fitting sleeves ended just below the elbow with turned-up cuffs; the chemise sleeve and ruffle edged in lace appeared below. The petticoat was worn over a structure called the 'capula' or 'bell hoop' made of distended hoops of whalebone or cane. The round-eared cap was worn, and being bonnet shaped, framed the face with the frilled front border. At the back, the cap was made to fit by pulling a draw-string.

The man wore the outdoor garment or greatcoat known as the redingote. The heavy cloth redingote was full but was pulled in at the waist with the assistance of a belt; the pleated flaring skirt reaching below the knees. The fastening was double-breasted. The neckline was encircled by two deep flat collars. The straight sleeves had very deep turned-back cuffs to elbow depth. The square-toed shoes had a long, high tongue which rose in front of the ankle. The tricorne hat was worn over a powdered bag-wig, which had a large bow at the back.

63 Lady and gentleman in Highland costume, c. 1745

This plate depicts the wrap-over gown without hoops, but with the full ruffle sleeves and a modesty piece. The lady is seen wearing the tartan screen or plaid, often worn by Scottish ladies to show their Jacobite sympathies. It was very popular in Scotland during the eighteenth century. The hair was fashioned in the style of the Dutch coiffure.

The gentleman is wearing the complete Highland costume of coat, trews and plaid. The jacket buttoned down the front, was hip-length and had a turn-over flat collar. Around the neck was worn a white stock. The trews were close-fitting breeches with the kneebands buckled below the knees over the stockings. From the right shoulder was a broad leather crossbelt which supported a claymore type sword on the left side. Encircling the waist was a black leather belt which secured the dirk dagger in front. Over the left shoulder was slung the plaid, or wrap-around cape. The fashionable bag-wig was worn. The tartan shown on this plate is the black and red of the Rob Roy tartan.

In 1747 the English Government passed the 'Dress Act' which made it illegal to wear or put on the clothes commonly known as Highland clothes. To disobey this Act meant six months imprisonment for the first offence and transportation to the colonies for seven years for the second.

64 Lady in a quilted petticoat, c. 1745

This dress of silk damask was in the open robe style, the most popular style of the period. The costume consisted of a bodice joined to a skirt which was open in the front to show the petticoat. Although its name implies an undergarment, it was in fact part of the costume and never hidden from view. The close-fitting bodice ended slightly below the normal waistline, and was lightly boned. It was open in front, with the edges bordered with short robings from around the neck over the shoulders to the waistline, and down either side. The opening of the bodice was filled in with a decorative stomacher, heavily embroidered with ribbon and lace. The stomacher was usually attached under the robings by pinning. The costume was worn over an oblong hoop which was flattened both front and back. The sleeves, which ended just above the elbow, were straight and close-fitting with small winged cuffs; the chemise sleeve ruffles emerged below. The petticoat was pleated onto a waistband and tied behind, it then fell in loose irregular folds to the ground. This particular petticoat was quilted to give both fullness and warmth. Long elbow-length gloves were worn. Over the head was a pinner, a lace bordered cap worn on the crown of the head. The lappets were turned up and pinned to the crown with a brooch or a jewel hat ornament.

65 Fashionable lady with embroidered robings, c. 1750

This was a typical fashion of the 1740–50s. The bodice had a widespread *décolletage* with robings laying over the edge of the shoulders. The plain stomacher was also wide. The robings crossed the back and came down either side to finish at the waist. Around the edge of the robings and across the top of the stomacher was a narrow lace frill or tucker. The sleeves were full to the elbows, then finished with three horizontal pleats, usually stitched down. From under the sleeves appeared the full sleeves of the chemise with deep double ruffles. High elbow-length gloves enclosed the lower arms. The skirt was worn over a dome-shaped hoop. The Dutch coiffure was worn, which consisted of the front hair waved back from the forehead, and the ears just visible below the hair at the temple. At the back there were a few ringlets at the nape of the neck; these were entwined with a ribbon knot. Over this hairstyle was a pinner which rested on the crown of the head; the lappets were drawn up to the crown and pinned up.

66 Madame de Pompadour, c. 1755

The sack gown, called by the French *robe à la française*, was worn at this period as an open robe, both for formal and informal use. The close-fitting bodice was open. The robings went round the back of the neck, over the shoulders, and then carried on down to the hem of the gown. The gap in the open bodice was filled by a stomacher with a series of ribbon bows, decreasing in size down to the waist. These were known as *échelles*. The stomacher was attached by pins to the tabs which were fastened under the robings. The sleeves ended just above the elbows and were close-fitting to the arms. They were decorated with a spreading ribbon knot at the elbow. Appearing below the sleeves were deep treble ruffles of lace which ended at about mid-arm. The overskirt and the petticoat adapted themselves to the type and shape of hoop worn. This gown had the dome shape. The supporting petticoat was usually made of buckram, the required shape being formed by distended hoops of whalebone or cane. It was attached around the waist by a draw-string. The petticoat was flounced and furbelowed. A lace ruff was worn round the neck. The hair was brushed back from the forehead and temples, the hair at the back being brushed up and formed into a small bun on the crown of the head. Pearls and ribbon often decorated the bun.

67 Guards Officer with lady, c. 1758

The lady wears the open robe gown with a trained overskirt, to which was joined the bodice. The robings crossed the outer edge of the shoulders and carried on down to the hem of the overskirt. The broad stomacher was trimmed with *échelles*, or bows, decreasing in size down to the waist. The stomacher was usually fastened to the robings by tabs which projected for this reason. The sleeves, which fitted well into the back of the bodice, were tight-fitting, ended at the elbows and were decorated with large ribbon knots. Ruffles trimmed with frills of lace extended from the sleeves. Around the wide square-necked *décolletage* and around the shoulders was crossed a chiffon 'handkerchief' which was fastened at the bosom. The petticoat was closely pleated into a waistband and tied at each side, falling into loose folds to the ground. It was trimmed with inverted flounces at about knee level. The popular elbow-length gloves were worn. The simple styled 'milkmaid' hat of natural straw was worn squarely on the head over the low insignificant coiffure.

The officer wears the dress uniform of the 1st Battalion of the Guards Infantry Regiment of the Prussian army. The chief characteristic was the evenly spaced rows of large loops and buttons which decorated the front and cuffs of the coat. The white gaiters were worn for summer uniform only. The hat was ornamented with silver lace and white ostrich plumage around the top.

68 Lady in 'bergère' hat with gentleman officer, c. 1760

The gown worn by the lady was made in a delicately patterned brocade. The wide *décolletage*, square in shape, was covered by a crossed 'handkerchief'. The short, tight sleeves fitted well into the back of the bodice, and finished just above the elbow with deep treble ruffles which reached almost to the wrist. The 'bergère' or 'milkmaid' straw hat was very popular at this time.

The gentleman officer wore the loose-fitting *justaucorps*. The coat fastened from the neck to the hem with buttons. The sleeves were straight with deep cuffs that were closed all round and ornamented with buttons and button-holes. Just below waist level were low-set pockets with deep flaps. The frilled shirt sleeves extended from the coat cuffs. A sleeveless waistcoat was worn; it was single breasted. The closer fitting breeches which fastened at the knees were becoming more popular and long woollen stockings were worn under the knee-high riding boots. The military black stock was worn forming a high neckband. For military gentlemen the 'pig tail' wig was often worn. The queue was long and spirally bound with black ribbon, and usually tied with black bows above and below. The three cornered hat was the accepted head wear. This, for the military, was broad brimmed, high cocked, and trimmed with a cockade. Around the waist was a sword belt supporting a military sword.

69 Lady and gentleman, c. 1760

The lady is wearing a close-fitting cap of white muslin. Her gown, in the sack-back style, is made of patterned silk. Short, tight sleeves end with a lace band with treble flounces just above the elbow. Deep treble frills of chiffon and lace hang from the band. Worn over the front is a white muslin apron.

The gentleman is wearing the *justaucorps*, which hangs loosely from the chest. The cuffs are ornamented with buttons and buttonholes. The waistcoat is sleeveless and usually knee-length.

The breeches, now became slightly closer-fitting than previously, with the waistband fastened by three buttons in the front.

The stockings are of either cotton or silk. The black leather shoes are round-toed and fitted with an oblong metal buckle.

1760-1789

70 Lady and gentleman dancing, c. 1765

The lady's hair is a mixture of real and artificial hair, and powdered all over. She wears a *robe à l'anglaise* with the *fourreau* or sack back. The square *décolletage* is edged with ruching and decorated with a bow. The open bodice is worn with a stomacher with a buttoned, false front.

The overskirt is worn over an oval hoop and has a little train at the back. The lady's petticoat is flounced. She is wearing satin-covered shoes.

The gentleman is wearing a wig with two horizontal rolls. The coat is similar to that illustrated in Plate 69, although the waistcoat is shorter. The breeches, too, have changed little since 1760, but they are somewhat tighter-fitting. He is wearing clocked silk stockings and gold-buckled shoes made of black leather.

71 Lady and gentleman, c. 1770

The lady's sack gown has a square-cut *décolletage*. The bodice has a boned lining and lacing across the stomacher. The sides of the skirt are pleated. The sleeves are well set in and are fairly close-fitting to just above the elbow. The back of the dress is made up of two double box pleats either side of a centre seam.

The gentleman is wearing the popular black tricorne. The satin coat is close-fitting and slopes away from the buttoned fastening on the chest. The skirt of the coat comes down to just above the knee. The back vents are trimmed with sham button-holes, while the coat is embroidered with gold lace. The waistcoat is single-breasted, cut away at an angle just below the waist. The breeches are also made in satin. He is wearing silk clocked stockings and shoes.

72 Lady in a tasselled Polonaise court gown, c. 1775

This glamorous lady is wearing a tall, narrow powdered Pompadour wig with four horizontal curls on either side of her head, and a vertical curl hanging behind her ear. At the back are two sets of four ringlets.

The overskirt is bunched up in three puffed-out draperies, uncovering the petticoat completely. The bodice is without robings, has a low, square neckline and fastens at the bosom with a bow. At the back, the bodice is shaped to the figure and continues into a flared skirt. In front, the laced waistcoat finishes in a blue point. The sleeves are elbow-length with round cuffs which are puffed and puckered, and tied round with ribbon. As an accessory she is carrying a hand-painted, ivory-handled fan.

73 German fashion, c. 1786

The lady's hat is ornamented with feathers, a muslin bow and streamers. She is wearing the open-robe style of dress with a tight bodice. The waistline is high. The sleeves are three-quarter-length, ending with a frill just below the elbow. The overskirt is trained and pleated to the bodice. The petticoat is long.

The gentleman is wearing the simple toupée. The coat has a turned-down collar in a different colour, to the coat. The sleeves are fairly close-fitting, ending in a small, round cuff. He is wearing the short waistcoat, vertically-striped and closed at the waist. His breeches are tight-fitting and long in the body and legs. Round his neck he wears a muslin cravat. Striped stockings and low-tongued shoes complete his outfit.

74 Lady in basque jacket with gentleman, c. 1789

This lady is wearing a white muslin mob-cap with a full crown. The close-fitting *basque* jacket has a longer, drooping back which protrudes over the fullness of the back of the skirt. The sleeves are frilled just below the elbow and a muslin *fichu* is draped over the shoulders. The full skirt is of patterned satin and reaches the ground. Her shoes are made of silk fabric. She is wearing a velvet wrap, edged with lace.

This gentleman is carrying a tall, beaver hat. His frock coat has tails which end at the back of the knees. The square-cut waistcoat is short, and its revers are turned over those of the coat. His breeches are stuffed into the jockey-type, black leather boots. The neck-cloth, made of lawn like the shirt frill, is wound around the neck, the ends forming a bow.

1789-1794

75 Lady and Muscadin, c. 1789

The French-style chemise gown, worn by the lady, is made of patterned muslin and tied at the waist. A muslin fichu is draped across the bodice. The front fall of the skirt is pleated on to a band for tying around the waist. The close-fitting sleeves end at the wrist with a chiffon frill. The hat is a large, mushroom type of white muslin.

The Muscadin has a tall, narrowing crown and a curling brim. He is wearing the claw-hammer-tail frock coat with a high, square cut-away waist. Close-fitting sleeves taper at the wrists. The lace-edged cravat fastens through the stand-fall collar. The square-cut waistcoat finishes at the waist. His breeches fasten at the knee with ribbon loops. His black jockey boots come to just below the knees.

76–77 Walking-out fashions, c. 1790

The general characteristics of the dresses illustrated are a tight bodice with a *buffon* (neckerchief), a round, high waist pleated to the waistband of the bodice, and a long, full skirt reaching to the ground with a small bustle. The *décolletages* are low and round. Sleeves are long and tight, ending with a small chiffon or lace frills, or just buttons. The ribbon girdles are buckled or buttoned either in front or to one side. Hairstyles varied during this period but the most popular are those with the fringe in front and ringlets round the back and sides of the head, below which the hair hangs, curled at the ends, either to just below shoulder length or almost to the waist, where it

is arranged and tied with ribbons. The hats are made of muslin and ribbons or, in some cases, are simply bandeaux of broad ribbon.

Male coiffures are now unpowdered, in the main fairly thick, reaching the collar, brushed back from the forehead and bushy with low side curls. The frock coat in various cuts and colours, either single- or double-breasted is worn. Waistcoats are now shorter and breeches fasten just below the knees with buckles or, in the case of the dandy, with ribbons. Stockings are worn with flat-soled, black leather shoes with silver buckles. Both the tricorne and tall beaver hats are illustrated. Fobs are worn and canes are carried as accessories.

78 Gentleman in the 'Werther' mode with lady, c. 1792

The gentleman is wearing a tall hat which is flat-topped with a tapering crown and a wide brim. A tricolor rosette is fixed at the top. The under-waistcoat has a shawl collar which appears just over the revers of the square-cut, single-breasted waistcoat, and his jacket is the long-tailed, double-breasted frock coat with a wide gap between the revers and the stand-fall collar. His breeches are of cassimere (a form of cashmere) and fasten with hanging ribbons. He wears the English-type jockey or top boots.

The lady's hat is tall with a soft crown. She wears a closed robe dress, the bodice of which has a low *décolletage* and the sleeves long, close-fitting and buttoned at the wrists. The skirt is gathered at the waist, falling full to the ground.

79 Muscadin in redingote frock coat with lady in redingote, c. 1792

The lady's hat is in the 'chimney-pot' style, with a large, round brim turned up at the sides. She is wearing the redingote dress in the open-robe style. The bodice is close-fitting with a falling collar and pointed revers. The sleeves are long and tight-fitting, buttoning at the wrists. The overskirt falls away on either side to reveal the petticoat.

The Muscadin wears a high-crowned, felt hat. His redingote fastens with self-material loops and buttons. The shoulders are covered with a double-falling collar and double-pointed revers. The coat sleeves are tight-fitting with loop and button closure. He is also wearing a lawn neckcloth, knee breeches with ribbon loops and jockey boots.

80 Ladies in walking-out summer dresses, with gentleman, c. 1793

The ladies are wearing the open robe with a *capuchin* collar. The bodice is fastened in position at the waist. The back has the narrow-cut look produced by setting back the sleeves.

The lady on the left has a trained overskirt which is parted from the wrap-over and makes a wedge-shaped gap in the front.

The gentleman wears a coat, made of a fine-faced cloth, close-fitting and single-breasted. His shirt and his cravat, which is tied at the front in a bow, are both made of lawn. He is wearing a buttoned-up waistcoat and his knee-breeches are of nankeen cloth. His stockings are a light-coloured silk and he is wearing fashionable, flat-soled shoes with gold buckles. In his left hand he is carrying an ebony cane.

81 Lady in a pierrot jacket with gentleman, c. 1793

The *à la conseilleur* coiffure worn by the lady is puffed out and frizzy with ringlets hanging down the back. Her round muslin hat is decorated with feathers and ribbons. The *pierrot* jacket is close-fitting with a low *décolletage* and short basques. The handkerchief is draped around the shoulders, *buffon* style. The skirt is gathered in at the waist and falls full to the ground.

The man carries a tall, crowned, black felt beaver hat. The frock coat has a stand-fall collar with metal buttons and tight-fitting sleeves with small cuffs. His waistcoat is double-breasted with pointed revers, and his breeches end just below the knees. He is wearing a lawn neckcloth tied into a bow, clocked silk stockings and flat-heeled, black leather shoes adorned with ribbon bows.

82 Patriots wearing Phrygian caps, c. 1793

The drummer is wearing a short peasant jacket called a *carmagnole*. His *pantalons à pont* open in front by means of a panel which is held in position with three buttons. The red felt Phrygian cap is upright with a pointed crown and ornamented with red, white and blue tricolor cockade of the French Revolution.

The other figure is also wearing a Phrygian cap with the tricolor cockade, a *carmagnole* and a redingote. The revers and short collar are in a red cloth. The length of his *pantalons à pont* is governed by the height of his jockey boots, which are highly polished black leather with light brown leather turn-downs and boot straps hanging on either side. He has a tricolor sash of the French Revolution over his shoulder.

1795-1804

83 Lady in riding habit, c. 1795

The riding-coat dress, as the name suggests, was originally designed for riding, but it became very popular as a morning walking-out dress. The close-fitting bodice has pointed revers in front, similar to those on a man's greatcoat, and the neck is encircled by two falling collars. The neckline is very low and the lady is wearing a *buffon* (neckerchief). The dress has a full skirt to the ground and is fastened with buttons right down the front. The lower buttons can be left undone, showing the petticoat. The sleeves are long and tight and fasten at the wrists with buttons.

84 Gentleman and lady in walking-out dress, c. 1800

Here is the male fashion at the beginning of the nineteenth century: a high-waisted, cut-away coat, tapering sleeves and pantaloons (trousers). Two cravats are worn, one in black and the other, which is underneath, in white. The gentleman wears the beaver top hat.

His partner is wearing the neo-classical type of dress in a light, clinging muslin with a rounded *décolletage*. It has short, puffed sleeves, is high-waisted, and has a separate train attached to the centre back by hooks. The skirt falls to the ground and the sleeves are full-length. The lady's hat is a silk bonnet-type, with a piping of contrasting silk around the back and the brim, and is edged with ribbon bows which form the strings for tying under the chin. She carries a fan.

85 Lady in a spencer with gentleman, c. 1800

The gentleman's top hat is made of beaver with a slightly roughened surface and a large, tall crown, widening towards the top. The coat is cut away at the waist with long narrow tails and has sleeves which are puffed at the shoulders and tapered towards the wrists. The starched shirt frills stand well out from the chest with the points of the collar reaching the cheeks from under the high neckcloth. His loosely-fitting culottes end above the ankles.

The lady is wearing the classical dress – a high-waisted muslin chemise gown with a low *décolletage*, and a corded belt and tassels around the waist. Her gown is trained. She wears a velvet spencer, with a high-standing collar without revers. Her bonnet-type hat of tucked silk has lace frills and ribbons.

86 English officer and lady, c. 1801

The officer wears a cut-away scarlet tunic. The collar is high-standing, with a button loop of silver lace on either side, and open in front to reveal the black stock and small white *jabot*. The jacket is double-breasted with the revers turned back, showing their colour. The collar, cuffs and revers are in the 56th Regimental facing colour, purple. The epaulette is of silver lace with silver tassels. A crimson sash is worn around the waist. White kerseymere culottes, coming to just below the knee are worn, and black leather boots with reinforced tops. The headdress is the fashionable bicorne.

The lady is wearing the pseudo-Greek classical gown worn over a slip of thin taffeta. A separate train, falling to the ground, is attached at the back. She is wearing long gloves.

87 Ladies' summer walking-out dresses, c. 1804

These ladies are wearing the high-waisted, round gown style of the Empire. On the left is a girl in the long, light gown, full to the ground. She wears a deep embroidered bertha and high standing collar of lace-edged muslin, pleated round the neck. Around the high waist is a ribbon sash ending with a bow at the centre back. A frilled trimming at the centre back extends from the waist to the hem. The sleeves are short and slightly puffed and she is wearing three-quarter-length gloves. In her hand she has a *capote*.

The other lady is wearing a high-waisted long, light muslin gown. The sleeves are short puffs. She is wearing a straw, bonnet-shaped hat edged with satin frills, and three-quarter-length gloves. Over her arm she carries a shawl.

88 Lady and gentleman in walking-out dress, c. 1808

The lady has a high-waisted dress with scallop-edged epaulettes and short puffed sleeves. Around her neck she is wearing a stand-falling ruff. The centre of the dress, from the neck to the hem, is embroidered. On her head she is wearing a close-fitting hat made of ribbons and flowers.

The gentleman wears a double-breasted, square-cut coat. The pockets of the coat are at waist level, and the sleeves are close-fitting, slightly puffed at the shoulders, with plain cuffs. A stand-up collar is turned down at the neck and a starched wing collar reaches the cheeks. His accessories include a fob and he carries a cane.

89 Lady in riding costume, c. 1808

The lady's riding habit is still very much in the Directoire style, having a *capuchin* collar cut low in front. The small waistcoat has revers which overlap the collar of the short-waisted jacket. The skirt is long and voluminous, so that when she is walking the lady has to carry it over her arm. She is wearing a lawn shirt with a frilled front and a masculine full cravat tied in a knot in front. She wears a version of the male top hat which has replaced the Directoire jockey hat. Her hair is styled in classical ringlets and she has short, thin leather gloves.

90-91 Ladies and gentlemen in walking dress, c. 1810–13

The gentleman on the right follows the Brummel fashion, with the skirts of his coat cut back to form a square-cut tail-coat. The high, stand-fall collar has low-turning revers with M-shape notches. The jacket is double-breasted with five brass buttons. The collar of the shirt rises high against the cheeks and turns up all round. A lawn cravat wraps around the neck and ties in a small knot in front. His trousers, which fasten under the shoe, are high-waisted, with a slight fullness at the hips tapering down to the ankles. He is wearing slippers trimmed with small buckles.

The other gentleman also has a square-cut tail-coat, with a button on each of the deep vents, and outside pockets at waist level. The sleeves are narrow and long with slightly gathered shoulders and

small rounded cuffs. The front of the single-breasted jacket, which fastens with only three buttons, slopes away from just above the waist. He is wearing high-waisted, close-fitting pantaloons which fit boots and a high shirt collar and cravat lying close to his cheeks. He is carrying a beaver top hat and leather gloves.

The lady on the right is wearing the classical, high-waisted, vertical gown with a high neck and deep muslin ruff. The untrained skirt is ankle-length with a slightly-flared hem. The sleeves are long and close-fitting. Her bonnet-type hat is ornamented with feathers and ribbons.

Her companion is wearing a similar high-waisted, ankle-length dress, but with a low *décolletage*. The sleeves are short and puffed.

92 Gentlemen in redingote and garrick redingote, c. 1814

The gentleman on the left is wearing a double-breasted, knee-length redingote with hip-level, horizontal, flapped side pockets and fairly close-fitting sleeves. It is fastened from the neck to just below the waistline with two rows of buttons. The back of the coat has a vent with two buttons in the centre. He is wearing top boots and a top hat with vertical sides.

The other gentleman is dressed in the all-enveloping, loose-fitting garrick redingote with several collars. It fastens down the front and is fitted with drawstrings and buttons and straps to alter the girth if required. The turned-up collar or cape can be closed at the throat with a strap and button. The vertical pockets have buttoned-up flaps. The brim of the gentleman's top hat turns up on either side.

93 Lady and gentleman in evening wear, c. 1815

The gentleman wears a frock coat and tight-fitting breeches, silk stockings and pumps. The shirt collar stands upright, touching the cheeks, and the neckcloth is in the form of a cravat. The waistcoat is of white-embroidered, white satin. Features of the jacket include revers and a stand-fall collar. The skirts of the coat reach almost to the back of the knees. This gentleman is carrying his bicorne.

The lady's evening dress is the still popular, high-waisted Empire style. Hem frills are now very much in evidence and both the sleeves and the hem are *appliquéd*. The lady's feet peep out beneath the shorter skirts. Her headdress is decorated with feathers. Her short puffed sleeves are set off by elbow-length, coloured gloves and she is carrying a matching fan.

94 Lady and gentleman in spring costume, c. 1818

The gentleman is wearing a well-fitting long *surtout* or greatcoat which is padded from the shoulders to the chest, is single-breasted and reaches to the ankles. The collar and lapels are also reinforced with padding. The gentleman is wearing a high shirt collar with the points touching his cheeks, and a cravat. He is wearing the ankle-length pantaloons. He is wearing a tall hat with the crown widening slightly at the top. He has ankle boots and cotton gloves.

The lady is attired in a high-waisted, high-necked, ankle-length dress flared out at the bottom. Over this she wears a *pelisse*. The sleeves are puffed and end at the wrist with a lace frill. Draped around her shoulders is a patterned silk shawl with tasselled borders. She has a large muslin poke bonnet.

95 Two ladies in morning dress, c. 1820

The lady on the right is wearing the redingote *pelisse* with straight, long sleeves and a simple *pelerine* or tippet which has a double collar of vandyked tulle or gauze. The front of her skirt and the base of her gown are trimmed with bands of gathered muslin bows. The brim of her silk poke bonnet curves to frame the face.

The other lady is wearing a slightly newer fashion. Her shoulder line is dropped and the waist, covered with a ribbon sash, is now back in its natural position and smaller than previously. The style of the sleeves is *gigot* (leg-o'-mutton). The *canazou* is of ruched tulle. The skirt of the gown is wide and completely exposes the ankle. Flowers and ribbons decorate the wide-brimmed poke bonnet.

96 Ladies in winter fashion, c. 1822

The full cloak worn by the lady on the left falls to just above the ankles. The collars, the front and the hem are trimmed with fur. Her dress is high-necked with a collar frill, a natural waistline and an ankle-length hem. The sleeves are *demi-gigot,* partly covered by elbow-length gloves. The hat brim is now wavy and in a poke bonnet shape.

The lady on the right is wearing a mantle trimmed with fur at the wrist. The upstanding collar and the hem are both made of wide fur and around her shoulders she is wearing a fur shawl. The bonnet, decorated with feathers, is funnel-shaped with falls on either side of the face and ribbons knotted under the chin. The border is ruched in silk and blond lace inside, framing the face. She carries a muff.

97 German and French costumes, c. 1826

The German lady on the left is wearing an ankle-length dress, which has a pleated bodice with a lace-edged, round neckline. The dress is frilled from the knee to the hem, and a buckled belt encircles the waist. The sleeves, puffed at the shoulders, taper down to the wrists and end in a frill. Feathers and ribbons, which dangle down on either side, decorate her large hat. She is wearing kid gloves.

The French demoiselle is wearing a similar dress and a French shawl of flowered silk, with deep borders. Her hat is very large and heavily ornamented with flowers and ribbons. She carries a decorative parasol.

98 Lady and gentleman in walking-out costumes, c. 1826

The gentleman's double-breasted frock coat has a rolled collar, full skirts to knee level and horizontal pockets with flaps. The sleeves, which are slightly gathered at the shoulders, are long and close-fitting with a slit in the cuffs. The trousers are strapped under the boots. He is wearing a top hat with the brim turned up slightly at the sides and a crown which widens at the top.

The lady's dress, trimmed from knee level to the ankle-length hemline, has a high neck with a turn-down frill, and a buckled belt at the waist. The sleeves are *demi-gigot*. She is wearing white kid gloves, and her hat is very large with a profusion of ornamental feathers, and ribbons which fall to the waist.

99 Lady and gentleman in outdoor dress, c. 1829

The lady's dress has a draped bodice with a *fichu*. The neckline is high and the collar is gathered on a band and secured with a ribbon around the neck to form the ruff and small cape. A buckled belt is worn round the waist. The dress is slightly funnel-shaped and is frilled from the knees to the ankles. The *gigot* sleeves are full at the shoulder and then taper to the wrists. Her hat is very large and trimmed with broad ribbon. Over her shoulders is a shawl.

The man is wearing a single-breasted frock coat. The tails reach down to the knees. The sleeves are close-fitting with *gigot* shoulders. The trousers are full at the waist and taper down to fasten under the foot. On his head is the topper with the brim turned up at the sides.

100 Lady and gentleman in day dress, c. 1830

The lady is wearing a wide dress, above ankle-length. The bodice has a V-shaped front formed by converging pleats from the shoulder to the waist. The *gigot* sleeve is full at the shoulder, tapering to the wrist and has a small turn-back cuff. Two capes cover the shoulders. The bonnet hat has a very wide brim edged with satin. On her feet she wears low-slippered shoes.

The gentleman is wearing a double-breasted frock coat with a velvet collar and large revers. The waist is tight-fitting as are the sleeves. The skirts are square-cut, ending just above the back of the knees and the trousers are styled *en matelot*. His satin neckcloth has collar points touching the cheeks. He wears a tall silk hat and carries a cane.

101 Lady in riding costume, c. 1831

The riding habit, popular both of necessity and because it was considered attractive, was often worn as a breakfast dress as well. The one illustrated is made of a coloured waterproof cloth. The tightly-fitted jacket, with short revers and a velvet collar, is decorated with buttons down the front. The skirt is extra full to allow it to sit properly when the wearer is mounted on horseback and underneath, *tricot* drawers are worn which fit tight over the instep and are held in place by a strap passing over the riding boot. The sleeves are in the *gigot* style. The masculine top-hat, of silk or coloured beaver, has a dark-coloured gauze veil which floats behind in the breeze. A fashionable masculine-style neckcloth ties in front in a bow and is worn with a white ruched shirt front.

102 Lady in 'pelerine en ailes d'oiseau' with gentleman, c. 1833

The lady's dress has a close-fitting bodice with a fairly low *décolletage*. It is fitted with *gigot* sleeves, over which lies the *pelerine en ailes d'oiseau*. The ankle-length skirt is full-gathered at the waist and puffed out with petticoats. The bonnet is made of silk, the crown of which is decorated with flowers and ribbons.

The gentleman is dressed in a double-breasted tail-coat. The sleeves are close-fitting and have slit cuffs. He is wearing two waistcoats; the top one is made in a beautiful silk brocade. His goffered shirt has a high collar and the cravats are low. The tight-fitting trousers are held in position by a leather strap. He is carrying a wellington top hat.

103 Lady and girl in walking-out costumes, c. 1834

The close-fitting bodice of this lady's dress has ruching right down the front to the hem. The sleeves (*imbecile* sleeves) are very *bouffant* coming full to the wrists and fastening in a tight cuff. The skirt, too, is very full and puffed out with starched petticoats. Her silk bonnet has a tall crown. She carries a parasol as an accessory.

Her little girl is wearing a close-fitting bodice with the waist encircled by a wide ribbon sash tied in a bow. The *pelerine* is edged with ribbon. The skirt is full and comes just below the knee while the overskirt is ruched and edged with ribbon. The cambric trousers or pantalettes are similarly decorated. She is wearing gaiter boots.

104 Lady and child in summer costumes, c. 1836

Summer wear for the lady consists of a dress with a close-fitting bodice and tight, elbow-length sleeves. A cape-like collar called a 'bertha' accentuates the sloping shoulder-line. The neckline has a turned-down, frilled collar tied in a bow at the centre. The full skirt is gathered at the waist and falls to the instep. She is wearing a large bonnet, decorated with feathers. She carries a parasol as protection from the sun. The little girl is wearing a tight-fitting bodice and a full skirt. The pantalettes can be seen hanging down below the dress and fastening at the ankles.

The gentleman in the background is wearing a petersham frock coat, short and full. It is double-breasted with a broad velvet collar and sleeves tight to the wrists. He is also wearing double waistcoats.

105 Gentleman in short redingote with lady, c. 1836

The lady is wearing a high-necked, close-fitting bodice with a small turn-down collar and filled neckband. The skirt is full, pleated on to the waist and long to the ground. These 'Victoria' sleeves are tight at the shoulder but are wide and very *bouffant* at the elbow. The bonnet, bedecked with feathers and ribbons, has a wide brim.

The gentleman is dressed in a tight-waisted, short redingote or frock coat which has rather tight sleeves, flaring skirts, large, wide revers and a velvet collar. It is thigh-length and closes with two rows of buttons. The trousers are tight-fitting and fasten *sous pieds*. The shirt collar is high on the cheeks but is kept in place with a small cravat. He is carrying a top hat with a rather high crown, and a walking stick.

106-107 Walking-out costumes, c. 1838

The top of the dress worn by the lady on the right is made up entirely of large shawls which are bordered with deep lace and draped to the figure. One is draped across her shoulders, others hang over each arm and another forms the collar. They give the appearance of one large shawl or mantle. The skirt of her gown is flounced around the hem. Her 'drawn' bonnet is made of gauze and silk on a wire frame.

The lady on the extreme left is wearing a dress cut low off the shoulders, which are covered by a bertha. The bodice fits close to her figure. She has a *capote*-style bonnet, decorated with an upright feather, which has a flower-pot style crown and a wide brim framing her face. Ribbons tie under the chin in a bow and the ends dangle down loosely. Her hairstyle is sleek with a centre parting and a bun. She wears cotton stockings and kid gloves.

Next to her is a lady wearing the *pelisse* of cape collars, which follows the shape of the shoulders, fastens with ribbon ties down the front and merges into the 'Victoria' sleeves. The bodice is tight-fitting, and the skirt, the hem of which has a wide trimming, is gathered at the waist and falls full to the ground. She wears the *capote*-style bonnet with a *bavolet*.

Their male companion has a double-breasted tail-coat, close-fitting to the waist with a shawl collar, and a knee-length cape with the collar turned down. His trousers fasten *sous pieds*. His hair is curly and he has whiskers and a moustache. His 'Cumberland' top hat completes the outfit.

108 Family group, c. 1839

The gentleman's short redingote has a slightly flared skirt and a deep collar of velvet trimmed with braid around the edges. The trousers are tight-fitting and strapped under the shoes. He is wearing a cravat and silk top hat and carries a cane.

His wife has on a morning open-robe dress with the long-waisted, figure-hugging bodice. Her sleeves are tight to the wrist where they turn back in a small cuff. The long skirt touches the toes of the shoes. It is trimmed from waist to hem with brandenburgs. It is gathered at the waist and made very full by the bustle and many petticoats. She has a *passe-étroite* bonnet decorated with feathers. She carries a fringed shawl. Their little boy is in a velvet coat and pantalettes hang from under his coat to his ankles.

109 Ladies and young girl, c. 1840

The lady has on a summer morning round gown. The long-waisted bodice is draped with folds to form a V-shape to the waist. The neckline is half-high and has a ruching decoration. The sleeves have the earlier *'mameluke'* variation of gauze *bouffants*. The full skirt reaches to the ground and has two deep flounces edged with lace. The bonnet she is wearing is now almost horizontal with the brim and crown in one.

In the background is a lady with a close-fitting jacket bodice and waistcoat buttoning down the front and revealing the open bodice chemisette, pleated and laced. The skirt is separate.

The little girl is wearing a close-fitting bodice with a square neckline. The skirt is full and wide, mid-calf length, with deep flounces. Stockings and silk gaiter shoes are visible.

110 Two ladies in day dresses, c. 1842

The dress worn by the lady on the right has a long-waisted, figure-hugging bodice, boned in front. The *décolletage* has a high V-shaped opening. A deep falling border covers the top of the sleeves which are in the Victoria style. The skirt is full to the ground and gathered into the waist. The top hair is brushed sleekly down from the centre.

The lady on the left is wearing a morning dress with a close-fitting bodice and a net *pelerine* which has a V-shaped neck with a deep, turned-down collar, and which fastens down the front to join at the pointed waist. The sleeves are tight to the wrists. The bonnet, with a *bavolet*, is set back a little on the head and trimmed with lace and ribbons, which tie under the chin in a bow.

111 Lady and gentleman in autumn costumes, c. 1842

This lady has a long-waisted, close-fitting bodice coming to a point in the front and fastening at the back. It has a high, closed corsage and wide, straight, three-quarter-length sleeves with lace cuffs, from under which come *engageantes*. The skirt is long and full, gathered at the waist and decorated down the front with wide lace trimming and ribbon bows. Her *pelerine* is also trimmed with lace. She is wearing a bonnet decorated with feathers. Her companion wears a Chesterfield *paletot*. It is slightly waisted, reaching just above the knees, and single-breasted. The side pockets are without flaps. His waistcoat is single-breasted and has a shawl collar. He has on a scarf-neckcloth and his trousers are tight-fitting and fastened *sous pieds*. The top hat is slightly curved out at the top.

112 Indoor and outdoor costumes, c. 1843

The lady on the right is wearing an outdoor redingote dress with a bodice cut close to the figure. The collar is deep with wide revers and the sleeves are tight to the wrist. The habit shirt is encircled by a turn-down collar. Her dome-shaped skirt is long and full to the ground and gathered in at the waist. Her bonnet frames her face and the ribbon strings emerge from the inside of the brim.

The other lady is dressed in an indoor dress. The close-fitting bodice is draped across the front with folds from the shoulders meeting in a V-shape in the centre. The sleeves are three-quarter-length and edged with lace. The long skirt falls to the ground and has five flounces. Her front hair is brushed smoothly down from a centre parting.

113 Lady in day dress with boy, c. 1846

The morning dress worn by this lady has a close-fitting jacket bodice, buttoned down the front from neck to waist and finishing with short *basques*, and a lace *basquin* overhanging the skirt. Encircling her neck is a lace collar and she has elbow-length sleeves lying over her Victoria sleeves. The skirt is long to the ground, gathered at the waist and organ pleated. She is wearing a ruched silk bonnet with a *bavolet*. Her hair is parted in the centre with ringlets. The young boy's single-breasted, short jacket has a narrow turn-down collar, and buttons all the way up. The sleeves are tight to the wrist. His trousers are without a crease and ankle-length. He is wearing slipper shoes and carrying a round straw hat. His hair is curly all over.

114 Gentleman's frock coat, c. 1846

Illustrated are front and back views of the frock coat. The double-breasted jacket is long and narrow-waisted and fastens with a button stand, the skirts ending just above the bend of the knee. The low collar joins the very wide revers with a V-shaped notch. The long sleeves are close-fitting and end in short cuffs fastened with buttons. The waistcoat is single-breasted, long-waisted and buttoned from the neck to just below the waistline. The shirt collar is high and the cravat has fringed ends. The trousers are wide, becoming narrower towards the ankle, and are fitted with straps under the instep. A silk top hat is worn.

The back view shows the cut of the coat and the two back pleats, which fall from just below the waist on either side.

115 Lady and gentleman in walking-out costumes, c. 1848

The lady is wearing a large *mantelet à pelerine*, embroidered round the edges with a deep lace frill; the closed, round neck is encircled with a deep, falling, double-lace collar. The skirt is gathered at the waist and long to the ground. The bonnet is the popular type with crown and brim horizontal, and a *bavolet*. Ribbon strings fasten under the chin in a bow with dangling ends.

The gentleman wears a double-breasted *paletot*. It reaches just above the knees, and is buttoned down the front. The turn-over of the wide revers reaches to the waist and reveals the double-breasted, square-cut waistcoat with flat revers and the top of his under-waistcoat. He is wearing a high collar with a cravat. The trousers taper at the ankle and fasten *sous pieds*.

116 Lady in frilled bonnet with small boy, c. 1849

The lady is wearing a three-quarter-length silk shoulder wrap, deep at the back to cover the bustle, and the front closes to the neck. The cape is embroidered. The dress underneath has tight sleeves to the wrist. The skirt is long and full. She has on a silk ruched cap with a *bavolet*.

The little boy is dressed in the tunic form of jacket where it is gathered slightly, and reaching to just above the knees and buttoned down the front. Around the waist he wears a broad belt. Beneath the tunic he has pantalettes with frilled edges, which fall just below the knees. On his head he wears a felt, bowler hat.

The man in the background is dressed in a morning coat with a silk top hat, and he is carrying a walking-stick.

117 Lady and girl of fashion, c. 1850

The lady's day dress has a *basquin* bodice, buttoned to the waist, with a V-neckline and a turned-down collar edged with a narrow lace frill. There are bell-shaped sleeves which reveal the sleeves of the chemisette which are puffed and fasten at the wrists. The skirt is full to the ground. Over her shoulders and arms she wears a large shawl with a fringed border. The bonnet is wide-brimmed, with a *bavolet*. The crown and brim are all-in-one. Her short day gloves are tight-fitting.

The little girl is dressed in the close-fitting, square-cut jacket bodice with a short *basque*. She also has the bell-shaped sleeves, with undersleeves. The skirt is long to the knee and flounced, and the pantalettes hang below the skirt to just beneath the knees.

118 Lady and young girl in day dresses, c. 1851

The lady is dressed in a day dress with a close-fitting bodice. The sleeves are three-quarter-length and end in a large ruffle. The skirt, gathered at the waist, is long to the ground, and just below knee length there is an ornamented border encircling the dress. She wears a muslin cap at the back of her head. The lady's coiffure has a centre parting with a chignon at the back of her head.

Her little girl is wearing a three-quarter-length shoulder cape, high to the neck and fastened down the front with braided loops. The dress beneath falls to just above the knees, and the lace-edged pantalettes just below. The legs are encased in long gaiters which button up the outside of the leg. The felt hat has a low crown and a wide brim.

119 Gentleman in a burnous with lady, c. 1851

The gentleman wears over his shoulders a three-quarter-length, cape-like overcoat called a burnous. It hangs straight and has a hood. He does not put his arms in the hanging sleeves. The trousers are tight-fitting and fasten *sous pieds*.

The lady has a close-fitting, redingote-style dress. The bodice is V-shaped and is filled in with the habit shirt with a small, turn-down collar around the high neck. The sleeves are close-pleated at the armhole, then full to the wrists. The skirt, *en redingote*, is full to the ground, ornamented up the front and on to the bodice, with buttons from just above the waist to the hem of the skirt. Over her arms she is carrying a large shawl. Her silk-covered bonnet has a lace *bavolet* and is decorated with a feather.

120 Ladies in crinolines, c. 1855 with young girl, c. 1852

On the right of the picture is a lady wearing a jacket bodice which fits closely to the waist, with *basques*. The neck is closed with a lace collar and she has open sleeves with *engageantes*. Her skirt is wide and full with treble skirts. Her day cap is far back on her head.

The other lady is wearing the bodice with the *basquin* body and short *basques*; it is closed to the neck and fastens up the front. The open sleeves have *engageantes*. The skirt is very full with scalloped edges. The cap sits on the back of the head. The little girl has on a tight-fitting bodice with a chemisette high to the neck and a deep epaulette collar. The sleeves are bell-shaped to the elbow with large, turn-back cuffs with undersleeves. The skirt is triple-flounced.

121 Lady in crinoline with young boy and girl, c. 1856

This day dress has a waist-level bodice and a high neckline with a lace, turn-down collar. The *basque* of the jacket hangs over the wide, flounced crinoline skirt. The sleeves are the bishop type. On her head she wears a *fanchon* bonnet.

The boy is wearing a jacket bodice with a *basque*. Bell-shaped sleeves reveal the full chemise sleeves which emerge from underneath and are puffed to the wrist. The skirt reaches just above the knees and short pantalettes hang down from underneath. He has cotton stockings and gaiter-type shoes. He wears a round-peaked cap and is holding a stick and hoop. The girl's jacket bodice has a square neckline and short, puffed sleeves. The *basque* of the jacket stands out over the wide hooped skirt.

122–123 Day and evening dresses, c. 1857

The lady on the extreme right is dressed in an evening gown with a bodice which is deep-pointed at the waist. The *décolletage*, trimmed with lace, is set off the shoulders, and the V-shaped front is trimmed with wide lace revers. The short sleeves are hidden under epaulettes of lace. The overskirt is gathered at the waist and very full, reaching to just above the knees, while the skirt underneath is decorated with small flounces and flowers and falls to the ground. Her hair is ornamented with flowers and she has on elbow-length gloves.

Next to her is a young lady with a tight bodice coming to a point covered by a ribbon bow. The bertha (collar) is wide over the shoulders, diminishing to the centre waist, and the V-shaped *décolletage* is filled in with a chemisette. The sleeves are short and *bouffant* with a ribbon bow. The skirt is full to the ground.

Centre is a lady in a redingote day dress, shaped to the waist with

a wide-based skirt falling full to the ground. The dress buttons from the neckline, which is encircled by a narrow, turn-down collar, to the hem. The sleeves are in the 'pagoda' style – tight-fitting at the shoulders, expanding to a wide opening just above the wrist, and worn with tight *engageantes*. A small hat is decorated with flowers.

Their male companion wears a three-quarter-length, double-breasted *paletot* which flares from the shoulders, has wide revers and braided arm slits. A small cravat is worn with the high shirt collar. His trousers are tight-fitting, fastening under his foot, and his silk top hat crowns the fashionable waved hair, worn with side whiskers.

124 Lady in crinoline with little girl, c. 1857

The gown worn by this lady is a day dress with a high-necked bodice fitting tight to the figure and fastened from neck to waist with buttons. The neck is encircled with a narrow, turned-down collar. The sleeves are in 'pagoda' fashion with triple flounces and attached *engageantes*. The crinoline skirt is full with five flounces varying in size. She has a cap with a *bavolet*. She wears gloves.

The little girl is wearing a tight-waisted bodice over which is a *mantelet écharpe* – a *pelerine* with long scarf ends hanging over the front of the dress. Her sleeves are 'pagoda' style with muslin sleeves underneath. The knee-length skirt is double-flounced and below hang the frilly drawers. Her hat is low-crowned. Her boots button up on the inside of her legs.

125 Young ladies of fashion, c. 1860

The young lady on the right wears a dress ornamented with ruching. The jacket bodice with short *basques* is closed round the neck with a narrow collar. Round her waist she has a buckled belt. The sleeves are the 'coat sleeve' type. The skirt is funnel-shaped with a wide base while the overskirt is a series of long *basques*.

The other lady is dressed in a tight-waisted overdress. It is single-breasted and buttons from the high neck to just below the waist. The straight sleeves are tight at the wrist and the neck is encircled with a small, turn-down collar. It is trimmed with gimp cord and the skirt is funnel-shaped with a wide base. The skirt underneath falls to the ground and is edged with a frill. Her bonnet is ornamented with flowers and ribbons.

126 Lady in travelling coat with small boy, c. 1860

The lady has on a travelling cloak-coat which is made of a light alpaca trimmed with ribbon. At the waist it is close-fitting but it then flares out in a bell-shape until it meets the dress, which continues the bell-shape effect to the ground. The sleeves are wide, full, bell-shaped, edged with broad ribbon and worn over a chemise with full, lawn sleeves fastening at the wrist. The hem of the dress is trimmed with a wide ribbon border. On her head is the 'spoon' bonnet, decorated with feathers and ribbon.

The little boy is dressed in a belted tunic, which has a rounded neck. The three-quarter-length sleeves have deep, turned-back cuffs. Underneath he wears a chemisette with full sleeves. He is wearing baggy knickerbockers with stockings and gaiter shoes.

127 Lady in Stuart cap with gentleman, c. 1862

The lady's walking-out dress has a bodice cut close to the figure and straight sleeves with an opening from under the elbow to the wrist, revealing the puffed chemisette lawn sleeve. The skirt is funnel-shaped with a very wide base. Her head is covered with the lace-edged Stuart cap.

The gentleman with her is wearing a long jacket coming about two-thirds of the way down the thigh. It is double-breasted, fastens high on the chest and has a narrow collar and revers. The plain sleeves are narrow and long to the wrist, revealing the edge of the starched cuff. A tie is worn. The trousers are baggy and rather shapeless except for a slight tapering from mid-calf to ankle. He is wearing a beaver top hat and he wears gloves and carries a cane.

128 Lady in day dress with small boy, c. 1862

The lady's day dress has a bodice and skirt cut in one. The bodice is tight-fitting and closed around the neck in a V-shape. The sleeves are bell-shaped with full chemisette sleeves underneath. The skirt is pyramid in shape, very wide at the base. Around the waist is a sash. The spoon-type bonnet has a straw brim and the face is framed in a lace cap. She is carrying a silk parasol and a straw boater.

The boy is wearing a three-quarter-length dress. It is shaped slightly at the waist, and flares out over the crinoline support to just above the knees. The sleeves are elbow-length and reveal the full chemisette sleeves of lawn which are wrist-length. The chemisette is closed around the neck with a small turn-down collar. He is wearing pantalettes.

129 Lady with mantilla and lady with bolero, c. 1863

The lady standing is dressed in a tunic dress with a bodice buttoned down the front to the fitted waist. The high neckline has a small turn-down collar. The overskirt is joined to the bodice and falls into a 'key' shape which reveals the underskirt. A deep epaulette covers the long sleeves which end in a wrist cuff of lawn. The lace bonnet lies flat on the head.

The seated lady is wearing a separate bodice and skirt. A bolero with deep, lace-trimmed epaulettes is worn over the sleeves. The skirt is full and funnel-shaped with a very wide base. Around the waist is a broad buckled belt. The bonnet, in *fanchon* style, has a silk caul with lace decoration. From the *bavolet* at the back hangs a veil. She is carrying a silk parasol.

130 Ladies in riding habit, c. 1865

These ladies are dressed in the fashionable riding habit. The close-fitting bodice comes to a V-shaped point in the front and is buttoned from here up to the high, rounded neckline. The sleeves are straight with a turned-back cuff, closed with two buttons and edged with the same thin lace frill that appears round the neck and down the front of the bodice. This bodice is gathered on to the voluminous skirt, giving an even greater effect of fullness. They are wearing masculine, silk top hats with muslin veils which fasten round the base and hang down the back, almost to the waist. The lady in the foreground carries a riding crop.

1870-1900

131 Young ladies in evening gowns, c. 1873

The young lady on the right is dressed in a ball gown with a low, round, off-the-shoulder bodice in the *polonaise* style, edged with a frill. Attached to the bodice is an overskirt, looped up at the sides. The underskirt is long and trained and, like the overskirt, heavily flounced. The lace-frilled sleeves are very short and puffed. She is wearing short evening gloves of silk and carrying a fan.

The bodice worn by the very young girl has a round neck with a lace collar, and is attached to the overskirt which is trimmed *en tablier* in front. The short, puffed sleeves are decorated on the shoulders with ribbons. Round her waist is a broad ribbon sash. She is wearing long evening gloves, and around her head is a bandeau of ribbon.

132 Lady in a day dress, c. 1876

The main figure illustrated is in a walking-out day dress which has a jacket bodice with a long *basque* forming the overskirt. The waistcoat front is in a different material and has a V-neckline filled in with a chemisette which is fitted with a high ruffle collar. The sleeves are three-quarter length, fitting tight to the elbows and ending with large frilled cuffs. The long, trained overskirt is caught up at the sides, and the front falls into pleated draperies, *en tablier*. The hair is worn low over the forehead with a frizzy fringe. The straw hat has a small crown adorned with ribbon trimmings, and a wide brim; it ties under the chignon, then forms a shawl-shape surrounding the neck. She is wearing long suede gloves with eight buttons, and carrying a coloured parasol and a large fan.

133 Ladies in sailor and 'Princess' styles, c. 1876

The lady on the left is wearing a walking-out seaside costume. The high-necked, jacket-type bodice is hip-level at the front and sides. Both the jacket and the *basque* are decorated with wide trimming and buttons, and two rows of trimming form a sailor collar. The sleeves are also trimmed. The skirt has a tie-back fanned out in a short train.

The other young lady is dressed in the 'Princess' style, with the close-fitting bodice and double skirt. It has a square-cut neckline, which is filled in with a chemisette with a frilled *jabot*, and is high at the back. The long sleeves have deep, turn-back cuffs edged with a small frill and decorated with buttons.

134 Ladies in walking-out dresses, c. 1879

The lady on the left is wearing a dress with a hip-length jacket bodice. The *décolletage*, filled in with a frilled collar of lace, is V-shaped. The sleeves are elbow-length and have a turned-back cuff with a ruffle of lace. The skirt is double, the overskirt is turned back to reveal the silk lining.

She wears long day gloves and carries a small handbag made of silk with metal clasps. Her hair is worn with a fringe and is covered by a 'Rubens' hat.

Her companion has on a day dress with a matching coat. The tight-fitting bodice is buttoned right down to the hem at the hips. The neck is encircled with a small lawn collar, and the sleeves are straight to the wrist. The trained skirt is trimmed with ruffles and bows.

135 Ladies in evening gowns, c. 1880

The lady on the left is wearing the *cuirasse* bodice with a square-cut *décolletage*, high at the back of the neck. The front panel (*plastron*) is in a different material. The sleeves reach the elbows and end with ruffles. The skirt is long and the overskirt is caught up at the sides and draped in the apron fashion. The puffing of the sleeves and the puffing at the back of the skirt is in a matching colour to the shoulder lace and *plastron*. She is wearing drop earrings and gloves.

The other lady also has on a corset-shaped *cuirasse* bodice, high at the back with a square-cut *décolletage*. The *plastron* ends at the hips in a point. The sleeves are elbow-length, ending with a ruffle. The skirt is trained, and the overskirt hangs down the front. She is wearing fairly long, buttoned evening gloves.

136 Lady and gentleman in evening wear, c. 1881

The lady's evening gown has a *cuirasse* bodice coming to a point in the front. The low *décolletage* is off-the-shoulders and ornamented with a deep lace and velvet *fichu*. The sleeves are short and puffed, with velvet ribbon and bows. The skirt is trained and flounced, and decorated with lace and velvet ruching. The overskirt is also flounced and trimmed with large velvet bows and a sash of velvet.

The gentleman has on the square-cut dress-coat evening suit. The skirts are narrow at the bottom. The sleeves are close-fitting with a turn-back cuff. The single-breasted waistcoat has a deep V-shaped front. The trousers are narrow with a braid running down either side from the waist. The evening shirt has a high, closed collar and a small cambric bow-tie. He is wearing plain white gloves.

137 Lady in tailored dress and waisted jacket, c. 1881–2

The main female figure is clothed in a tailor-made jacket with matching skirt. The jacket is close-fitting, especially over the hips, and has wide revers and collar. The tight sleeves end at the wrists with a turn-back cuff. Around her neck she has a lace collar with dangling ends, fastened by a brooch in the centre. The skirt is draped, caught up at the side, slightly trained and decorated with fringing. Her waved hair has a centre parting and a short fringe; the side hair is taken back into a 'Cadogan' style at the back, exposing the ears. She is wearing a *toque* hat ornamented with white doves' wings and flowers which stand well up in the air. She is carrying gloves and a parasol.

Other costumes can be seen on the background figures.

138–39 Walking-out dress, c. 1885–7

The lady on the extreme left wears a jacket bodice with long, close-fitting sleeves. The overskirt is drawn up at the sides and bunched up at the back. Her hat is decorated.

Next to her is a man in the background wearing an Ulster (long loose overcoat), checked cape, and a high-crowned bowler hat.

The gentleman in the centre is wearing a single-breasted morning coat. The waistcoat is cut straight, and the shirt collar is high and worn with a neck-tie. His trousers are close-fitting and narrow at the bottom. He is carrying a bowler hat, and a walking-stick.

The next lady is dressed in a jacket-bodice dress.

To her right are two background gentlemen: one is wearing a double-breasted, reefer-type jacket with a low, straw hat; the other

is wearing a morning coat and a top hat.

The background lady is wearing the tailor-made habit jacket with tight sleeves. The hat is decorated with birds, feathers and ribbons.

The lady on the extreme right is in a close-fitting jacket bodice with small revers and a deep collar, buttoned from neck to hem. The *cuirasse* bodice is cut slightly higher at the hips to make room for the drapery. The front of the jacket is long and the back covers the top of the bustle. The sleeves are close-fitting down to the wrist with a wide turn-back cuff fastened by three buttons. The overskirt is straight in front, drawn up at the sides, then draped towards the back. The skirt hangs to the ground in pleats. She is wearing a bonnet and carrying a parasol.

140 Ladies in evening gowns, c. 1887

The lady on the right is wearing the *cuirasse* bodice with the *plastron* in a different colour. The *décolletage* is square-cut and surrounded by a deep lace collar high at the back and falling over the shoulders. The sleeves are elbow-length, ending in a frilled ruffle. The overskirt is drawn up at the sides and draped at the back. The dress is decorated with ribbon, ribbon bows and lace.

The other figure is dressed in a *cuirasse* corset bodice with a square-cut *décolletage* filled in with a frilled collar which is high at the back and has a V-shaped front. The sleeves are elbow-length, ending in a frill. The overskirt is draped, showing the skirt beneath as a wedge piece prettily decorated with lace. The coiffure has a fringe, and is brushed back to reveal the ears.

141 Lady in bustle dress skating costume, c. 1888

This lady is wearing a hip-length jacket, close-fitting to the waist, long in the front, and up at the back over the bustle. It is trimmed with fur around the neck, down the front and then around the hem. The sleeves are close-fitting and long to the wrist with a fur cuff. The skirt is draped with kilted skirts over the bustle. She is wearing the high-crowned bowler and suede gloves.

The man is dressed in the tunic-type hip-length jacket which has straight, close-fitting sleeves, and which buttons from the neck to just below the waistline. It has a closed, round, high collar. His breeches fasten at the knee with three buttons, and he has woollen stockings, gaiter-type skating boots and an astrakhan round hat.

142 Lady in walking-out dress with gentleman, c. 1893

This walking-out dress of the early 1890s has a short jacket fitting close to the figure at the waist, and a wide turned-down collar and revers. The leg-o'-mutton sleeves are finished off with small, turn-back cuffs. The jacket, open in front, reveals the shirt blouse with its softly-fitted front. The felt hat has a wide brim, which is ornamented with ribbon and a stuffed bird with wings. The full bell-shaped skirt, with the centre panel edged with braid and ornamented with straps and buttons, reaches the ground.

The gentleman wears the popular lounge suit. The high-buttoned jacket fits fairly closely to the body and is braided. The trousers are creaseless and come well down over the boots. He wears the popular, high starched collar with a large tie.

143 Walking-out costumes, c. 1894

The lady's jacket is cut to fit closely to the figure, with the high 'Officer' stand-fall satin collar and wide satin revers. The bodice is cut in the 'Eton' shape and the cambric waistcoat is frilled down the centre. The skirt of the gown fits closely over the hips and falls in folds to the ground. The sleeves are full to the elbow, then tight to the wrist. The small bonnet is worn with small ostrich feathers.

The gentleman wears a high-buttoned frock coat, with a small round collar and short revers. The high, choker-type, starched collar is worn with a wide knotted tie. The trousers are not creased, and he has a black silk top hat.

The child is dressed in the popular sailor suit, dark stockings and ankle-boots. On his head is the round 'tam-o'-shanter'.

144 Ladies' evening dresses, c. 1895

The lady on the right wears a dress with a plain skirt edged with two narrow frills at the hem. It is made in crimped wool *crépon* with bands of velvet as ornamentation. The bodice is pleated and the square *décolletage* is trimmed with velvet. Around the waist is a velvet sash into which is sewn a concealed pocket containing a sachet to perfume the handkerchief.

The costume on the left is made of silk and lace. The skirt is bell-shaped at the bottom and the overskirt is a simple and effective draping. A wide ribbon sash is worn. The sleeves are the wide, *bouffant* leg-o'-mutton type, full to just above the elbow, then tight to the wrist. The cape covering the shoulders fastens in front beneath the centre pleat and is caught down each sleeve with a bow.

145 Lady and gentleman in street attire, c. 1895

The lady's costume is in sailcloth, with waistcoat revers and cuffs ornamented with mother-of-pearl buttons. The well-cut *godet* skirt is popular because of its graceful line, and combined with the jacket with a full, short *basque* forms a very fashionable ensemble. The pleated sleeves, which finish with elegant cuffs give the required width to the costume. Her beaver hat has a box crown.

The gentleman is in a morning coat with short revers fastened with three buttons above the waist. The skirts are longer and more cut-away. The high, stiff collar and cravat are still in fashion. The trousers are creaseless, pin-striped, and come down well over the shoes. The black silk top hat and light-coloured suede gloves complete the outfit. A cane or umbrella is carried with this outfit.

146 Lady in lounge gown with children, c. 1895

The dressing gown, or lounge gown as it is known, is worn by the lady 'at home'. It is made in velveteen and lace, with an overdress of cashmere. The front material is lined throughout and hangs loosely down to the feet.The weight of the gown is suspended from the shoulders. The bow securing the lace collar is sewn on.

The smaller child is dressed in a pinafore dress made in muslin and ornamented with lace and muslin embroidery. Both back and front have radiating rows of insertions.

The tall girl on the right is wearing an embroidered frock. The front is set in a double box-pleat up to the square, embroidered yoke. The silk sleeves and undervest are made up on a tight-fitting lining and they fasten at the back.

147 Lady and girl in summer dresses, c. 1896

The female costumes in *crépon* and silk are illustrated here. The skirt is ornamented at the waist with three cut-steel buttons. Each seam has a crossway fold of *crépon* and shot silk. Large *crépon* sleeves match the full, silk bodice. The back of the bodice is similar in design to the front. Each of the collars fasten at the centre with a group of bows. The hat is made of muslin and silk.

The young girl wears the new, much shorter length of coat for children in *piqué* with two box pleats back and front, and a square yoke fastened with mother-of-pearl buttons. The large collar and epaulettes are made in the new embroidered cambric. The sleeves are large and loose to make allowance for the puffed frock sleeves beneath. The hat is made of stiffened muslin and decorated.

148 Lady in home gown with young girl, c. 1896

This cashmere tea-gown has the 'Stuart' bodice, close-fitting to the waist. The wide collar terminates in velvet rosettes just below the bosom. The sleeves end at the wrists in a frill. The high-necked vest is of Oriental silk threaded with gold. The skirt falls to the ground, bell-shaped, and the hem, the collar and the sleeves are all embroidered in a lighter silk.

The young girl wears a velveteen, fur-trimmed dress, with a short-waisted bodice. The skirt fastens with three buttons of jet or steel. The cape collar comes to a point in the centre of the back and on either side of the shoulders and is set off by a satin necklet. The sleeves are full-pleated to the elbow, then taper and fit at the wrists. Her shoes match the colour of her dress.

149 Ladies in winter costume, c. 1897

Illustrated here is the long double breasted overcoat fastened with sixteen large buttons. The sleeves are cut in a new way, with a plain piece off the shoulders. The collar and neck-tie of satin sets off the coat nicely.

The lady in the background on the right is dressed in a cloth costume with the bodice cut away in front. The little velvet coat is finished with a *basque* at the back. The skirt is long and decorated at the hem. The boat-shaped hat is made of panama straw.

The lady on the left has on a gown of cloth with large sleeves to just above the elbows. Her hat is fairly flat with a small crown.

The man wears the still popular silk topper and three-quarter-length Chesterfield coat.

150 Lady and gentleman in evening dress, c. 1899

The lady is dressed in a corset-like, close-fitting bodice with a round waist. The *décolletage* is low and off the shoulder with large 'balloon', short sleeves. The skirt is trained with lace-trimmed side panels. Her hair is brushed back, high on the forehead in the Greek style, and exposing the ears. She has dark coloured stockings and dancing shoes with the Louis heel and long evening gloves.

Her male companion is wearing an evening dress coat with a plain collar and silk-covered revers. The skirts reach just above the knees and are spoon-shaped. His waistcoat is single-breasted with a narrow turn-back, and his trousers are trimmed with braid running down each leg. His hair is close-cut with a parting.

1900-1920

151 Ladies in walking-out dresses, c. 1903

The lady on the right is in a morning gown which has a loose, full bodice with a deep *fichu* dipping to a point down the back and over each shoulder. It is worn over the straight-fronted corset, which brings down the bosom line. The waist is very tight and the hips accentuated. The neckline is high and boned up the sides under the ears. The sleeves are full from the elbow and are gathered into a wristband. This lady is wearing her hair high over pads on her forehead. Her straw hat has a small crown and a wide brim turned up on either side.

The lady on the left is in the 'Grecian bend' silhouette style, with the loose bodice, high-boned neckline, the full bosom, the very slender waist, the full hips and the long sweeping skirt.

152–153 Ladies and gentleman in outdoor costume, c. 1909

The young lady on the extreme right is wearing a calf-length tailored coat, cut away round to the back. The coat is left open to reveal the close-fitting dress which hangs to the ground. The neck is encircled with a high lace collar and falling lace cravat blouse. The coat is embroidered with a design in braid. The sleeves are close-fitting and straight to the wrist. The coiffure is covered with an enormous hat with a large, soft silk crown and a large flat brim.

The background lady wears a high-necked, natural-waisted dress with a loose-fitting overblouse. The sleeves, are finished off with hanging three-quarter flounces. She wears a wide, flat, straw hat.

To her left is a lady in a green tailored day dress which is cut close to the figure. The dress is straight to the ground with ornamented

fastenings down the right-hand side. The *décolletage* is high and the neck is encircled with a muslin collar. The straight sleeves end just above the elbow. Over her fashionable coiffure she has on a high-crowned, large-brimmed hat.

The lady on the extreme left is dressed in a day gown with a loosely-cut, high-waisted bodice. The neckline is high and has a collar of small frills. The sleeves taper slightly to just above the wrists. A panel of a different material is set in the dress from just under the bosom to the ground. The hat she is wearing has a very high crown and is decorated with frills. Her hair is worn high on top.

The gentleman is in the widely-worn motoring costume in the 'dust coat' style. His cloth cap has ear flaps and a small peak.

154 Lady and gentleman in day dress, c. 1912

This lady is attired in a day dress with a bodice draped across the body to form a V-shape. The hobble skirt is very tight; a small *tablier* or apron is added as decoration. Her bolero jacket has short sleeves which have a turn-back cuff frilled with deep lace and end just above the elbows. On her head is a very large-brimmed hat with a trimming of standing feathers.

Her gentleman friend is dressed in a single-breasted morning coat, fastened in front with two buttons. It has a narrow collar and revers and he is wearing a stiff turn-down collar and a tie. Striped trousers become closer-fitting towards the bottoms. He has a silk top hat and carries kid gloves and a walking stick.

155 Ladies in day dresses, c. 1912

The lady on the right is wearing the draped-over bodice forming a V-front, which is filled in with a high-necked blouse and high-waisted tunic. The sleeves are close-fitting to the wrists, where they flare out slightly. The skirt is gathered in at knee-level, narrowing down to the instep. Encircling the waist is a sash. The hat has a large brim turned up straight all round.

Her friend is also wearing a draped-over bodice and a knee-length tunic. The Directoire high waistline is accentuated by the belt over the long, cut-away overblouse. The blouse is high-necked and the sleeves are long and close-fitting to the wrist. The skirt narrows from knee-level to the ankle. The hat is made of velvet and ornamented with feathers. She is carrying a fancy handbag.

156 Fashionable costumes, c. 1913

The main female figure is in a walking-out costume with the long, loose-fitting, three-quarter-length caped coat. The hem and the turn-down collar are edged with fur. At hip-level is a very wide sash. The sleeves end in a fur cuff. She is wearing the hobble skirt, slit at the sides and narrowing towards the ankle. Her felt hat is worn well over the head with the left side higher than the right. Attached to the brim is a spotted veil which covers the face completely. Her short gloves are made of suede and she carries a very large fur muff. The background figures are also in fashionable outdoor wear: on the right, the 'Zouave', fur-trimmed jacket and hobble skirt with the three-quarter-length overskirt; on the left a design after Poiret, with his strong Oriental influence.

157 Ladies and children in day dresses, c. 1915

The lady on the left is clothed in a high-necked, pleated bodice blouse with long bishop sleeves. Over this she is wearing a two-tiered, round-necked, pinafore dress. The skirt falls to eight inches off the ground. Her hat is small and round with a narrow brim. She is wearing two-colour high boots buttoned at the side.

The lady on the right is wearing an enormous tent-shaped coat with balloon-shaped sleeves and it has large, round patch pockets, one on either side. Her hat has a bowler-shaped crown.

The young girl is in a short, loose-fitting, knee-length dress.

The boy wears a single-breasted jacket. His V-necked waistcoat is worn with a turned-down soft collar and tie. His trousers are just knee-length. Both children are wearing boots.

158 Outdoor costumes, c. 1917

The lady on the right is wearing a loose-fitting tailored day costume. The bodice jacket falls to hip level and the neckline is V-shaped and surrounded by a wide collar. The bodice is fastened down the front and a belt encircles the waist. It has long, close-fitting sleeves with deep cuffs trimmed with buttons and braid. The skirt hangs down to eight inches from the ground and is trimmed with a pattern of braid and buttons. The velvet hat has a high crown and an undulating brim. She has high, two-toned boots.

The other lady has on a knee-length coat with a close-fitting bodice. The high V-shaped neck is encircled with a large fur collar which is high at the back to cover the shoulders. Straight sleeves end in fur cuffs. Her high-crowned hat is made of felt.

159 Ladies and young girl in afternoon dresses, c. 1918

The lady on the left has on a waistless loose-fitting dress above hip-level. The bodice has a natural shoulder line and round neckline. The sleeves are long and kimono shape to the wrists. The skirt is full at the hips, narrowing at the hem which comes just below the knees. Her hat, decorated overall, fits closely to her head and she is wearing gloves.

The little girl with the group is attired in a short party dress, finishing full just above the knees. The very full skirt, with a triple-flounced hem, is gathered at the waist which is encircled with a wide ribbon sash. The high, round neck is surrounded with a large collar coming over the shoulders, and the sleeves are the long, bishop type. She is wearing ankle-strap shoes.

160 Ladies in coats and dresses. c. 1920–21

The lady on the left is wearing a Russian-style, three-quarter-length coat with a high, round Cossack neck. The top is slightly fitted, flared slightly at the waist and fastened with buttons down the left-hand side. The sleeves are straight to the wrists and the narrow skirt falls to mid-calf. Her close-fitting hat has a high crown.

The centre figure has on an evening dress which has a loose, low, round-necked bodice filled in with muslin. It has short kimono sleeves ending in flounces high at the front. The skirt is full at the hips, narrowing at the ankles and elasticated to draw it in tight. Strings of pearls and feathers adorn the hair.

The figure on the right is attired in a tailored costume with a severe, rather masculine line.

1920-1939

161 Lady's evening dress and costume, c. 1921

The barrel-shaped evening gown of satin (left), designed by Erté (Romain de Tirtoff), came to ankle length, with a centre vent opening almost to the knee. The top section was cut in one piece with the sleeve. The sleeve itself was open from just below the shoulder to the wrist, caught there, and then continued over the hand. A contrasting coloured satin lined the open sleeve. The middle section was braided with soutache in various shades.

The figure on the right is wearing a two-piece costume consisting of a jacket and a calf-length fringed-hem skirt. The jacket, worn over a blouse, was open to the waist with a long lapel, and fastened with three buttons in front at hip level. A slim chain girdle was worn at the natural waistline. The sleeves were full to just below the elbow, then close-fitting to the wrist. Close-fitting hats were becoming popular at this time.

162 Evening clothes for fashionable men and women, c. 1922

The lady wears an elegant below mid-calf taffeta evening gown designed by Erté, fitting close to the figure. A deep *décolletage* was formed by crossed-over wide ribbon lapels which finished at the waist in front. The ribbon motif then continued down either side, in lengths of ribbon loops of graduating lengths, to mid-calf. Drooping down from the waist is a girdle of a garland of flowers.

The man is in 'tails', a name given to the formal evening suit. The suit was either black or a midnight blue, made of a worsted material, double-breasted, but always worn open. The front is cut away, while the back has a centre vent to the waist turning into tails which just covered the bend of the knee. The lapels are silk-covered. The stiffly starched shirt front in the form of a deep 'U' has a stiff winged collar which is worn with a white bow tie. A single-breasted white waistcoat was always worn. Grey box-cloth spats were often worn over patent leather shoes.

163 Day wear for men and women, c. 1928

With the raising of the skirt, legs became important in fashion. The manufacture of silk stockings reached a new art. The lady is wearing a one-piece day dress, a garment whose style at this time was dominated by straight, knee-length pleated skirts, with a low, hip-length waistband. The high round neckline has a turned down collar with long ties down the front. A coloured tailored coat was worn on top, slightly shorter than the dress. Popular was the high-domed, close-fitting cloche hat with a drooping brim turned down over the eyes. Furs became an important accessory: seen here is a natural fox fur stole with head, paws and tail. Court shoe styles were usual. Gloves and leather handbags were always carried.

The man is dressed in a smart double-breasted reefer jacket-type afternoon lounge suit, a style which characterised men's wear during this period. It has a well-defined waistline with three pockets outside – two hip and one breast – and a three-button cuff decoration. The straight trousers always had turn-ups. Suits were tailored from high-grade worsteds, saxonies, tweeds or flannel. Breast pocket handkerchiefs (foulards) were always carried at this period, and two-tone shoes (co-respondents) were popular.

164 Ladies' casual day wear and men's golf and leisure wear, c. 1928

Knee-length skirts dominated the fashion scene. Separate skirt and bodice, in the form of blouse or jumper, became very popular. The lady on the left is wearing a skirt with a godet front and inverted pleats. The loose-fitting jacket has a low neckline which reveals the blouse beneath. Sleeves were long to the wrist. The lady in the centre wears a knee-length skirt with knife pleats in the front. The hip-length jumper has a high neck opening. The sleeves are straight and close-fitting at the wrist. Both are wearing the popular close-fitting cloche-type hat.

Although used mainly for playing golf, these baggy tweed plus-fours were worn also as weekend leisure clothes. They often appeared in plain tweed or in gun-club checks, Glen Urquhart squares and many other designs. Brown, greys and beige were popular colours. For golf, jazz and Jacquard in knitwear were popular and the pullover became a universal cult. Golf stockings sometimes matched the pullover in colour and design, or were patterned in diamond squares and checks of all sizes. The cap in plain or checked cloth remained in fashion for all classes. Brogue shoes were always worn with plus-fours.

165 Day clothes for men and women, c. 1930

For women, the thirties brought in higher waistlines, longer skirts and a more mature and elegant silhouette. The popular cinema greatly influenced the main design of fashion. The lady is wearing a short jacket which hangs direct from the padded shoulders. Unfastened between waist and hip, it has wide revers and no pockets. The sleeves are in the bishop style, full from the shoulder and closing tight at the wrist. Beneath the jacket is a simple, matching-coloured calf-length dress. A close-fitting small matching hat is placed at a jaunty angle.

In the thirties lounge suits were redesigned to give a stronger, more masculine appearance. The waistline was set slightly above the natural line, and buttons and pockets moved up correspondingly higher. Lapels, shorter but increased in width, are seen here on a double-breasted jacket. Shoulders were built up, giving squareness to the shoulder line. Sleeves narrowed towards the cuff. The jacket fitted at the hips and was square-cut. Trousers were close-fitting at the waist, with turned up bottoms. Herringbone and small checks were popular.

166 Leisure wear for men and women c. 1934

Leisure was now more widely available for all classes, and the American designer Mainbocher designed this beachwear suit for women. This masculine type of design shows the 'workman's' smock, worn over loose bell bottom trousers flaring at the ankles. The design is based on the uniform worn by French railway porters. The hat, high-crowned, with a wide, floppy brim, was both practical and attractive. The popular bishop sleeve of the period was tight at the wrist. The loose, hip-length jacket was fastened by three buttons just below the neckline. Cretonne and cotton were amongst the materials that were most commonly used.

For casual or cruising outfits, the well-dressed fashionable male of this period usually wore smart, well-tailored, broad-shouldered, elegant, colourful striped blazers. These were usually single-breasted, as shown, but could be double-breasted. The trousers, or flannels as they were called, were close-fitted to the waist and could be in white, blue, grey or green. The novelty of zip fasteners for trousers was coming into fashion at this time. A coloured or striped cravat was always worn with these leisure clothes.

1939-1945

167 Women in uniform, c. 1939–1945

During the Second World War, women in uniform were accepted as a national necessity. On the left is a woman in the uniform of a British ATS corporal. The basic uniform was a khaki-coloured jacket and a below knee-length skirt of the same colour. The shirt, tie and stockings are in a lighter version of khaki. The uniform was always general issue. She wears a privately purchased forage cap, which carries the ATS cypher. The shoulder straps of the tunic bear only the letters ATS without the crowned wreath. There are four pockets – two hip, two breast – all buttoned. A self colour belt, attached to the tunic, girdles the waist with a brass buckle fastening in the centre. On either side of the upper arm are the white ranking chevrons. The shoes are the brown brogue type. She also carries the regulation gas mask slung from the right shoulder.

In the centre is a German Army Stabshelferin in field grey uniform. The unusual cut of the jacket shows the buttoned vertical pockets at the waistline. The breast pocket carries the eagle insignia on the rightside. The straight skirt has inverted pleats at either side. The field service cap (*Feldmütze*) is piped in yellow and black along the crown seam and in the front. Dark grey stockings and black shoes are worn. In the cylinder she carries the regulation German-type gas mask.

In the USA the Women's Army Service were dressed not in service-designated uniforms, but by the designer Philip Magnone. On the right is a WAC, SHAEF officer. She wears a battledress blouse (Ike jacket) with a piped yellow and black field service cap. Both jacket and cap are in a brownish olive drab. Silver bars on the jacket shoulder straps and the cap denote rank. Brass US cyphers are on the short narrow lapels, as is the Athena head, also in brass. The shirt and tie are in a paler shade of pinkish khaki. The straight, close-fitting, pale khaki skirt is knee-length. The shoulder patch is that of the Supreme Headquarters Allied Expeditionary Forces. The beige stockings and brown buckled shoes, also the shoulder bag, are regulation issue.

168 American and European women's day wear, c. 1942

The war years brought great austerity to the European fashion trade. On the right is a utility fashion of this period. It shows great simplicity of design, modelled on the battledress worn by service personnel. The tunic has wrist-length sleeves and short, wide lapels, and is fastened down the front by four large buttons. The skirt is cut straight to just below the knee. A coloured scarf or choker is worn. Hats were usually small, but with a jaunty look about them. Flesh-coloured stockings and low-heeled shoes were worn. A small shoulder bag completed the outfit.

American women fared better than those in Europe. Their clothes were more stylish, although they had a more casual approach to fashion. Everyday clothes were based on interchangeable separates: jackets, blouses, skirts and trousers. Small, fussy hats were very popular. Shown on the left is a very practical costume outfit comprising a hip-length single-breasted jacket with a long, wide lapel and straight sleeves with a turnback of a contrasting colour. The skirt is straight, below knee length, with a hip pocket in the same colour as the jacket. The high waistcoat with a centre fastening of buttons is in a contrasting colour to the jacket and skirt. Gloves and a shoulder bag were carried. Shoes of the popular court style are usually in the same colour as the main outfit. A small, close-fitting hat is worn, with a large veil covering the face.

1945-1960

169 Women's day wear: the New Look, c. 1947

With the ending of hostilities fashion began to pick up again. Dresses with longer skirts were designed, and Christian Dior created the New Look. This, as shown on the left, involved a tight waist, exaggerated hipline and much longer skirt. The natural line was achieved by removing the wartime padded shoulders. The fullness of the close pleated skirt was due to the number of petticoats worn beneath. The short, hip-length jacket was high to the neck with short lapels and fastened down the front with buttons. The waisted jacket flared out at the hips to accommodate the fullness of the petticoats and skirt, and had side pockets. The sleeves are straight, finishing with side buttons at the cuff. Ankle-strap shoes, as shown here, were very popular, as were sling-backs. Hats were large, plain but always elegant.

On the right, a design by Jacques Fath shows the popular style of the period. The full skirt of the dress hangs in heavy pleats with large side pockets. The dress bodice is high to the neck with a contrasting turn-down collar, and fastened from neck to waist by buttons. The close-fitting waistline is girdled with a wide, soft leather belt. Over all is a short, built-in bolero jacket with long, full sleeves to the wrist in a contrasting colour. A large hat with a full veil covering the face completes the outfit.

170 Teddy Boy and women's day costume, c. 1955

In the mid-fifties some male fashion designers moved backwards in time to create the Edwardian dandy fashion. This style became associated with delinquent teenagers and aroused great opposition, so Teddy Boy clothes, as they were known, remained firmly working-class. The jackets were long and single-breasted, draping to almost knee length, with narrow lapels reaching the chest; they fastened down the centre front. The jacket itself could be blue, red, yellow, maroon or black, while the collar, the four front pockets and the cuffs of the straight sleeve were edged in black velvet. Shirts were white, with long, pointed collars, and were worn with a long, narrow, 'Slim Jim' string tie. A single-breasted brocaded waistcoat, usually of a strong contrasting colour, was worn. Close-fitting drainpipe trousers, usually in a light colour, ended about ankle length to reveal the bright coloured socks. The shoes were thick crepe-soled, with strange names such as beetle crushers and brothel creepers. Hair was fairly long, well greased and brushed back to a point at the nape of the neck called the D.A. style.

In contrast, Marcel Fenez designed for women a close-fitting flared hip-length jacket with a narrow mandarin collar. The jacket was waisted with a centre fastening of three large buttons and had long straight sleeves to the wrist. The skirt was close-fitting to the figure and fell to calf length. The whole silhouette still retained the New Look cut. Hats were now usually small, round and flat, placed firmly on the head. Gloves were worn and handbags carried. Flesh-coloured stockings and the ever-popular court shoes were worn.

171 Women's evening and 'A' line day wear, c. 1957

This unusual cocktail dress designed by Givenchy shows a gathered puffball silhouette made up in the house of Christian Dior. The low *décolleté* off-the-shoulder style is tightly shaped to the bodice, and closes down the centre front. The sleeves are straight, closing at just above wrist length. The puffed-gathered skirt is drawn in at the waist, then pleated and puffed out at the front, back, and sides, and finally drawn in at calf length.

On the right is Christian Dior's famous design known as the 'A' line. The long to just below hip-length jacket fitted closely at the shoulders and flared down to the hips. The pockets are set low, to hip level. The jacket was double-breasted and decorated with seven buttons. The high neckline is closed with a narrow turned-down collar. The skirt is box-pleated and calf-length. The outfit is completed with a flowerpot hat, handbag and court shoes.

1960-1990

172 Women's day and evening wear, c. 1962–1965

The figure on the right shows the formal simple line in a shantung suit designed by Yves St Laurent. The hip-length waisted, unadorned jacket was high to the neck with a slight turnback of a lapel, and fastened down the centre front by five large buttons. The jacket had a small cut-away in the front. The sleeves were straight, reaching just above wrist level. The close-fitting mini-skirt reached just above knee level. A large felt hat and coloured gloves were the accessories of this fashion.

In the centre is an Italian fashion of this period designed by Emilio Pucci, noted for his printed fabrics. This strong Italian influence is characterised by the figure-hugging short-sleeved mini-dress with matching tights. The fantastic and unusual hairstyle was built up with hair and artificial braids.

The right-hand figure is wearing a simple evening dress with halter-type neckline. The bodice was close-fitting, while from the inverted V which came from mid-chest to the hips the skirt section fell away like a cone, widening at the ankle-length hem. The elegant hairstyle was typical of these times. Open sandal shoes were worn.

173 Modern art-inspired day dresses, c. 1965–1967

The search for new ideas in fashion continued in the sixties. On the left is a 'Pop Art' woollen jersey cocktail dress inspired by the American artist Andy Warhol and designed by Yves St Laurent. The simple, plain-coloured mini-dress has straight sleeves to the wrist. Against this plain dark background a Pop Art design has been *appliquéd* from the shoulder to the hem.

The wool jersey dress on the right was also designed by Yves St Laurent, but this time inspired by the abstract painter Piet Mondrian (1872–1944). The simple mini-dress was sleeveless with a high, round neckline and fell just above the knee. The popular Butcher's Boy cap was worn to complete the outfit.

174 Men's and women's styles, c. 1969

Designed by Cardin, centre, is a long-to-the-ground woman's maxi coat. The unusual collar was high to the neck which followed the same design to the waistline, finishing in a large, round, decorated fastener at the waist. The cuffs of the wrist-length sleeves and the hem of the bore had the same motif as the collar. Beneath she wears a hooded sweater, tights, and over them a very short mini-skirt. Black ankle-high boots are worn.

On the left, as shown in the 1967 spring/summer collection of Yves St Laurent, is a mini-length African-style dress adorned with shells and African jewellery which covered the bosom and hips, with see-through lattice-work at the midriff.

On the right is casual wear for a young man, showing the ideal male figure at this period. Tight trousers were worn low on the hips with zip-fastened leather jackets and coloured shirts. The contrived untidy hair was worn shoulder-length.

175 Women's fashions in modern synthetics, c. 1969

The vagaries of fashion followed all the avenues of newly invented materials. Here the new shiny vinyl-type fabric became an outlet for the high fashion of the period. The lady on the right wears a tailored mini-coat of vinyl material with a fitted waistline, short high lapels and double-breasted, with eight large buttons clustered from mid-chest to the waistline. The sleeves are straight and long to the wrist. Beneath would be a pair of close-fitting 'hot pants'. The legs to just above knee high are encased in close-fitting soft leather high boots, often of a contrasting colour.

On the left is a caped figure in long multi-coloured stockings and a vinyl high-necked cape falling to thigh level. This was an American fashion of the Art Nouveau Pop Art style invented by a graphic designer called Peter Max, who named it the Traffic Stopper.

176 Men's and women's day wear, c. 1970

On the left is a wide, leggy pyjama dress. The sleeves are long and close-fitting to the wrist, with bunches of strips of material hanging from the open slit shoulder. The neckline is high and square-cut. The footwear is *'a la Grècque'* and bound to the knee. The dress is close-fitting to the waist, flaring away to below knee level into wide-bottomed trousers, looking like a divided skirt.

On the right is a high-necked, short-sleeved, hip-length linen mini-costume. The plain tunic jacket has two side pockets indicated merely by the buttoned pocket flaps. A leather buckled belt encircles the natural waistline. The trousers are close-fitting and ankle-length. Hairstyles varied at this time. Here the style is a boyish close crop. A large brimmed hat with hanging decoration is worn.

The man represents the more formal style of this period and is wearing a coloured blazer-type jacket, double-breasted with long lapels. Trousers were in various colours, flared without turn-ups, and close-fitting at the waist. Shirts were in various colours, and a patterned cravat took the place of more formal neckwear. Hairstyles were often shoulder-length.

177 Denim and punk, c. 1977

Blue denim arrived on the fashion scene in the sixties and has remained in style in some form ever since. Although denim had been in use for a hundred years or more – it was invented in France, then used in America for miners', labourers' and children's clothes – its potential for fashion wear was recognised only in the early sixties when the unisex fashion of jeans arrived on the scene. Fashionable jeans came in a variety of colours from pale blue stonewashed to black. On the left is a young woman dressed in dark jeans and a denim jacket or blouse, under which she wears a tee-shirt. Unisex jeans always had fly fronts. On her feet she wears Howdy-Pardner high boots. Popular at the time were strings of rhinestones round the neck.

The man is wearing a denim outfit of jeans and shirt. Plain denim unisex designs were not intended to be chic: a great deal of effort was applied by the wearer to fade, shrink, or even fray them at the knees, hems and elbows, a trend expressed more aggressively in Punk fashions.

The young Punkette on the right is wearing a pinky-orange dyed Mohican roach or spiky stiffened hairstyle with exotic face make-up. Jackets were usually leather and often studded, with tee-shirts or string vests beneath. Black tights were worn, sometimes with the knees showing through. Mini-skirts in a variety of colours and even tartan were worn. Under high laced-up or crepe-soled boots went short ankle socks. Punks favoured bizarre jewellery. Arm and face tattoos were popular with both sexes. Bullet-belts, slung around the hips, were often added for further decoration.

178 Women's fashions, c. 1979

On the left is the elegant, sophisticated silhouette of a jumper-style blouse after a design by the Italian couturier Valentino. The blouse has a round neckline filled in by a soft silken cravat. The dark material background shows to advantage the horizontal and vertical braided stripes in a contrasting colour. The straight sleeves are caught closely at the wrists. Two side hip pockets are placed to fall in line with the ruching of the blouse at hip level. The thigh-length mini-skirt was broadly designed in vertical stripes, caught closely at the waist to allow the material to fall into wide pleats. Fine, flesh-coloured tights are worn with low-heeled pumps.

On the right is a design by Yves St Laurent. The main feature of this design was the *appliquéd* knee-length full skirt which flares out from the hips, showing to advantage Picasso's art. The top section consists of a close-fitting bodice with the waistline reaching to hip level. The three-quarter length sleeves are puffed at the shoulders, then straight to the elbow. The low, U-shaped *décolletage* is bound by an edging of a contrasting colour. The natural waistline is encircled by a broad, bowed girdle. Grey tights are worn.

179 Men's Casual and Woman's Fashion c. 1984 – 1990

Men wore casual fashion at this time, epitomised by this Giorgio Armani loose double-breasted jacket with a broad, sloping shoulder line and long lapels. Beneath the jacket a shirt is worn without a tie. The trousers are wide-cut, to give a slightly baggy look, and taper towards the ankle.

Short skirts became internationally popular in the late eighties. In the centre is a spectacular creation by Chanel: the skirt is thigh-length and close-fitting at the front, while at the back the material is formed into a bustle silhouette with a train. The neckline of the dress has a low *décolletage* enveloped by a large shawl collar. A stiff satin or taffeta, or any material which produced a rustling sound was used.

On the right is the 'Skimp' silhouette, designed by Yves Saint Laurent, with a high-to-the-neck, long-sleeved, figure-hugging jumper. The skirt is a thigh-length mini, straight and close-fitting with hip pockets on either side. A broad belt is pulled into a narrow waistline. Accessories consist of long contrasting gloves, which come well over the wrists, and a large, flat, circular hat. The outfit is completed by dark flesh-coloured tights and court shoes.

180 Women's formal clothes, c. 1990–2006

The lady on the left is wearing the Versace's geometric design style of evening dress with the striped material running across the body from the right to the left, diagonally from chest to waist, then running vertically from the waist to the hem. The upper bodice is a variation of the ubiquitous knitted theme.

The hair is long and allowed to fall over the shoulders.

The lady on the right is wearing the glamorous Lanvin ruched, closefitting, sleeveless dress. It has a plunging neckline, which is surrounded by a narrow black lace edging, with the ends falling below the knee and a bow at centre front. The bodice part of the dress is ruched to the hip level, then fallling into folds in the skirt. It is made in an opulent satin or silk with the highlights giving a glitz and glamour look. c.2004.

Index